GRAMMAR AND BEYOND

WORKBOOK

Lawrence J. Zwier
Harry Holden

2B

CAMBRIDGE
UNIVERSITY PRESS

University Printing House, Cambridge CB2 8BS, United Kingdom

One Liberty Plaza, 20th Floor, New York, NY 10006, USA

477 Williamstown Road, Port Melbourne, VIC 3207, Australia

314-321, 3rd Floor, Plot 3, Splendor Forum, Jasola District Centre, New Delhi – 110025, India

79 Anson Road, #06–04/06, Singapore 079906

Cambridge University Press is part of the University of Cambridge.

It furthers the University's mission by disseminating knowledge in the pursuit of education, learning and research at the highest international levels of excellence.

www.cambridge.org
Information on this title: www.cambridge.org/9780521279932

First published 2012
Reprinted 2018

Printed in Italy by Rotolito S.p.A.

A catalog record for this publication is available from the British Library.

ISBN 978-0-521-14296-0 Student's Book 2
ISBN 978-0-521-14310-3 Student's Book 2A
ISBN 978-0-521-14312-7 Student's Book 2B
ISBN 978-0-521-27991-8 Workbook 2
ISBN 978-0-521-27992-5 Workbook 2A
ISBN 978-0-521-27993-2 Workbook 2B
ISBN 978-1-107-67653-4 Teacher Support Resource with CD-ROM 2
ISBN 978-0-521-14335-6 Class Audio CD 2
ISBN 978-1-139-06186-5 Writing Skills Interactive 2

Art direction and layout services: TSI Graphics

Contents

UNIT
16 Future (1)

Life Lists

Be Going To, Present Progressive, and Simple Present for Future Events

1 Complete the radio interview about college students' life lists. Use the correct form of *be going to* with the verbs in parentheses. Use the negative when necessary.

Eric: Hi. I'm Eric Montoya. Today, I *am going to speak* (1) (speak) with Chelsea Barnes, an academic advisor at Woods Community College.

Chelsea, your college expects a lot from its students. What ________ (2) your students ________ (2) (do) to stay organized?

Chelsea: Well, it's pretty simple, actually. They ________ (3) (create) some lists.

Eric: OK. What kind of lists ________ (4) your students ________ (4) (make)?

Chelsea: Life lists.

Eric: What ________ (5) they ________ (5) (put) on their lists?

Chelsea: They ________ (6) (list) their goals. As college students, they have a lot of life goals, from passing an exam to training for a new career.

Eric: When ________ (7) you ________ (7) (get) the lists from them?

Chelsea: On October 31, the students ________ (8) (submit) their lists. Then I ________ (9) (meet) with them to discuss the lists. This is how we ________ (10) (find) ways to achieve each goal.

Eric: ________ (11) you ________ (11) (show) their lists to other people?

Chelsea: No, I'm not. These are private, so I ________ (12) (show) them to other students.

2 Complete the conversation about summer vacation. Use the form given with the verbs in parentheses.

Carolina: I'm happy that classes end today. I*'m going to enjoy* (1) (*be going to*: enjoy) the summer.

Drew: ________ (2) you ________________ (2) (present progressive: go) anywhere?

Carolina: Yeah. I ______________________ (3) (simple present: leave) for Brazil in a week.

Drew: Brazil? ________ (4) you ________________ (4) (*be going to*: visit) relatives there?

Carolina: Of course, Drew! I'm from Brazil!

Drew: Right. Sorry. I forgot. What ________ (5) you ________________ (5) (*be going to*: do) there?

Carolina: Well, I have a long list. First, I ______________________ (6) (present progressive: spend) a week with my cousins. What's next? Oh, right. On the 11th, my family and I ______________________ (7) (present progressive: have) a big barbecue. After that, I ________ (8) probably just ________________ (8) (*be going to*: rest) on the beach. What ________ (9) you ________________ (9) (present progressive: do)?

Drew: There's nothing on my list! I can't really go home to Hawaii. Flights are too expensive for me. So I ________ (10) just ________________ (10) (present progressive: work) part-time for a month or so.

3 Complete the newspaper article about a campus visit. Use *be going to*, the present progressive, or the simple present and the verbs in parentheses. Sometimes more than one answer is possible.

Dalton College News October 17

"Life List" Expert Visits Campus by Kelly Moore

Dr. Robert Shaver *is coming* (1) (come) to campus next week. Shaver, a psychologist, ________________ (2) (arrive) Monday afternoon for a five-day visit. Dr. Marta Sanchez, the president of the college, said, "This visit ________________ (3) (be) fantastic. Our students ________________ (4) (learn) a lot from Dr. Shaver." Shaver ________________ (5) (give) a public lecture, "Making Life Lists," next Thursday evening in North Hall. The event ________________ (6) (begin) at 8:30 p.m. "Shaver's lectures at other colleges have been very popular. Tickets for this lecture ________________ (7) (sell) out quickly," Dr. Sanchez said. Dr Vinh Tran of the Psychology Department said, "We all ________________ (8) (go) to the lecture." Shaver ________________ (9) (leave) on Saturday.

Avoid Common Mistakes

1 Circle the mistakes.

1. Hiro's life list says that he **is going to run** (a) in a race. He **going to start training** (b) next month. His parents **are going to watch** (c) him.
2. Tim and Jen **is going to get** (a) married. They **are going to buy** (b) a house. They **are going to live** (c) in this city.
3. What **you going to study** (a)? What job **are you going to do** (b)? Where **are you going to live** (c)?
4. **Is he going to go** (a) to college? **He going to study** (b) science? **Is he going to do** (c) research?
5. Jen **is not going to buy** (a) a car. Tim **is not going to buy** (b) one. They **is going to take** (c) the bus.
6. I plan to live where it **not going to be** (a) cold much, and it **is not going to snow** (b). I want a climate that **is going to be** (c) warm all the time.
7. Where **they are going to go** (a)? When **are you going to leave** (b)? How **is she going to get** (c) there?
8. My life list **is not going to be** (a) long. It **is not going to list** (b) many goals. I **not going to try** (c) many things.

2 Find and correct eight more mistakes in the article about a study on organization.

James University Study Needs Students

Researchers at James University is going to study how students organize their time next week on campus. They going to interview students about the ways that they keep organized. One question in the interview are going to be, "What you are going to do this week?" Another question is, "How you are going to plan your day today?" The interviews going to be in Building B. If you are interested, please sign up at the Student Services Center. Students is going to receive payment for their time. The researchers not going to tell the students the goal of the research. They is going to share their results in a report.

Self-Assessment

Circle the word or phrase that correctly completes each sentence.

1. Someday I _____ in a nice, big house.

   a. going to live b. am going to live c. live

2. Yi-Yin _____ her relatives in Singapore next month.

   a. am visiting (b.) is visiting c. visiting

3. Shannon likes making lists. In fact, _____ going to make a list of all her lists.

   (a.) she's b. she c. she goes

4. **A:** Where are you going to live? **B:** In Seattle. **A:** _____ there? **B:** No, it's not.

   a. Going to be cold (b.) Is it going to be cold c. When is it going to be cold

5. Do you plan to study mathematics? Where _____ go to college?

   a. you going to b. you are going to (c.) are you going to

6. I want to plan my classes for next semester. _____ with my advisor this afternoon.

   (a.) I'm meeting b. I meeting c. I are meeting

7. I got an e-mail from Brian about his plans. He _____ to Chicago to look for a job.

   a. is go b. goes (c.) is going

8. My class later today _____ at 3:00 p.m. and ends at 4:30 p.m.

   a. begin (b.) begins c. beginning

9. What _____ this summer?

   a. are you going (b.) are you doing c. you doing

10. Tim and Brian _____ in a dorm next year.

    a. not are going to live b. not going to live (c.) are not going to live

11. Pat plans to use her car less often. She's _____ a bicycle to work.

    (a.) going to ride b. going riding c. rides

12. Our men's soccer team _____ this afternoon.

    a. be playing (b.) is playing c. playing

13. According to their schedule, the band members _____ to Toronto next month to play in a concert.

    (a.) go b. goes c. going

14. You have to take this class, but it's not easy. _____ a lot of reading.

    a. You going to do b. Be going do (c.) You're going to do

15. Today, I'm meeting some friends for lunch, and then _____ a class at 2:00.

    a. I having (b.) I have c. I am

UNIT 17

Future (2)

Getting Older

Future with *Will*

1 **A** Complete the online tour website. Use *will* and the words in parentheses. Use the full forms.

SureTour for Older People: Wild Australia – North and South

Join us for a tour that *will definitely change* (1) (change / definitely) your life. Australia, with the world's oldest rocks and the most unusual animals, will definittelynot disappoint (2) (not disappoint / definitely) you. We understand that older travelers want new experiences. This SureTour will certainly not be (3) (not be / certainly) a typical, boring vacation. We'll take (4) (take) you where few travelers go. Our tour will begin (5) (begin) in Australia's far north. We'll land (6) (land) at Darwin International Airport on June 16. Then we'll travel (7) (travel) by bus to Kakadu National Park, home to hot jungles and hungry crocodiles. From there, we'll fly (8) (fly) to Australia's far south, the island state of Tasmania. "Tazzy" is famous for its healthy, clean environment – great for older travelers. Don't worry – you will probablynotmeet (9) (not meet / probably) a dangerous Tasmanian devil! You can enjoy easy hiking in Tazzy's beautiful hills.

Remember that June is winter in Australia, so we will possibly see (10) (see / possibly) some snow in Tasmania. We'll return (11) (return) to the United States on June 30.

B Write questions about the brochure in A. Use the questions and the words in bold to help you.

1. **Q:** *Who will run the tour?* **A: SureTour** will run the tour.
2. **Q:** *Will older travelers go on the tour?* **A: Yes,** many older travelers will go on the tour.
3. **Q:** Where will the tour go? (at DIA) **A:** The tour will go **to Australia's wild places.**
4. **Q:** When will they land? **A:** They will land at Darwin International Airport **on June 16.**
5. **Q:** How will they travel? **A:** They will travel **by bus.**
6. **Q:** What will they probably see in the park? **A:** They will probably see **jungles and crocodiles.**
7. **Q:** Where will the tour go next? **A:** The tour will go **to Tasmania** next.
8. **Q:** When will they return to the U.S.? **A:** They will return to the United States **on June 30.**

2 Answer the questions. Write sentences that are true for you. Use *will* or *won't.*

PAIR WORK

Breakout Rooms – write partner's answers, then report to another group.

1. How long do you think you will live?

   I will live for 100 years.

2. How will you stay healthy when you are older?

   I'll stay healthy by + ____-ing (gerund)

3. Where do you think you will live when you are older?

   I think I'll live + prep

4. Do you think you will work in your seventies and eighties?

   Yes / No

5. What will you do for fun when you are older?

   I'll ________ for fun...

6. Who will you spend time with when you are older?

   I'll spend time with ________

7. In your opinion, what will be some positive (good) aspects of getting older?

   IMO, some positive aspects will be + ____-ing (gerund)

8. In your opinion, what will be some negative (bad) aspects of getting older?

Future with *Will*, *Be Going To*, and Present Progressive

1 Read the sentences about saving for retirement. Check (✓) the correct reasons for using the verbs in bold.

1. Tomorrow, I**'m going** to a class. The class will focus on retirement planning.

   ☑ for an arranged event ☐ for a prediction, expectation, or guess

2. **I'm going to learn** about saving money now for retirement so that I have financial security.

   ☑ for an intention ☐ for something certain because of evidence

3. A lot of people my age **will probably be** at the class.

   ☐ for a planned future action ☑ for a prediction, expectation, or guess

4. Saving for retirement **will not be** easy.

   ☑ for a prediction, expectation, or guess ☐ for an intention

5. I spend a lot of money. It**'s going to be** hard to save any.

   ☐ for a planned future action ☑ for something certain because of evidence

6. This advertisement says that Jim Peters, a retirement expert, **is going to teach** the class.

   ☐ for a prediction, expectation, or guess ☑ for something certain because of evidence

7. This **is going to help** me achieve my goals for retirement.

   ☐ for a planned future action ☑ for a prediction, expectation, or guess

2 Complete the conversation. Circle the correct verb forms. Sometimes both verb forms are correct.

Lisa: Soon the Baby Boomers will be old. That **will affect / is affecting** (1) society a lot.

Alejandro: I'm sorry. I don't understand. Who **will be / is going to be** (2) old soon?

Lisa: **I'll / I'm going to** (3) tell you who. The Baby Boomers! They're people who were born after World War II, between 1946 and 1964.

Alejandro: Why **are they going to affect / are they affecting** (4) society so much in the future? Are they a big group?

Lisa: Big? It's huge! **I'm going to / I'll** (5) check this number later, but I think they're probably about 25 percent of the United States population.

Alejandro: Yeah. That's big. With that many, I can see that **they'll / they're going to** (6) have a big impact.

Lisa: Right, and maybe they **won't have / aren't having** (7) a positive impact.

Alejandro: OK. So **I'll / I'm going to** (8) guess what the problem is. **They're going to need / They'll need** (9) lots of health care.

Lisa: Definitely. OK, well, I have to go. I **am going to meet / am meeting** (10) my parents for dinner. See you later.

3 A Write the adverbs in the box in the correct columns of the chart.

certainly	~~likely~~	perhaps	probably
definitely	maybe	~~possibly~~	~~undoubtedly~~

Degree of Certainty		
← Less certain	← In the middle →	More certain →
possibly	*likely*	*undoubtedly*

B Rewrite the sentences with the adverbs in A that have the meanings of the words in parentheses. Sometimes more than one answer is possible.

1. (more certain) Baby Boomers are going to change our society.

   Baby Boomers are undoubtedly going to change our society.

2. (in the middle) According to predictions, 25 million U.S. Baby Boomers will retire by 2020.

   ____

3. (more certain) When the Boomers retire, companies won't have enough workers.

   ____

4. (less certain) Younger workers will make more money because companies need them more.

   ____

5. (in the middle) Some medical companies are going to get rich because Boomers will need medical care.

   ____

6. (more certain) For example, Boomers are going to need products to fix their old knees or hips.

   ____

7. (in the middle) A company that makes those products will do well.

   ____

Avoid Common Mistakes

1 Circle the mistakes.

1. In the future, people **will live** (a) longer. More people **live** (b) to 100. Millions **will be** (c) centenarians.
2. My grandfather **would possibly retire** (a) next year. He **will possibly get** (b) another job after that. He **will possibly have** (c) a second career.
3. We**'re going to visit** (a) a home for older people. You**'re going to enjoy** (b) it. They **going to tell** (c) some interesting stories.
4. Older people **will stay** (a) healthier. They **will to get** (b) better health care. Better medicines **will become** (c) available.

5. I **will to stay** (a) healthy when I'm older. I **will eat** (b) good food. Also, I **will exercise** (c) every day.

6. Older people **would possibly have** (a) money problems. Maybe Social Security **will not get** (b) fixed. They **will possibly need** (c) to keep working.

7. After retirement, you and I **will have** (a) fun. In our later years, we **travel** (b) a lot. We **will experience** (c) new things.

8. I **am going to plan** (a) carefully for retirement. I **going to save** (b) my money. I'**m going to retire** (c) before the age of 60.

2 Find and correct eight more mistakes on the website for seniors.

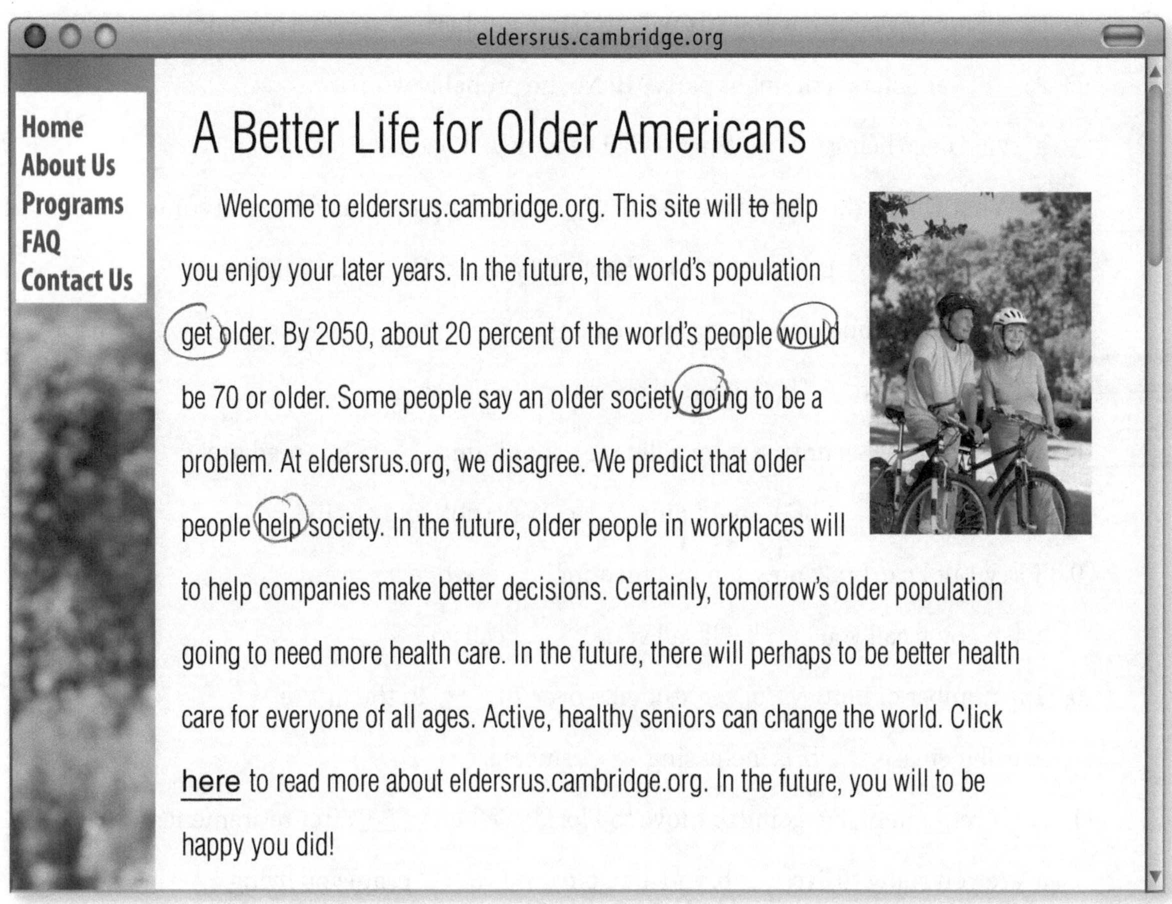

eldersrus.cambridge.org

Home
About Us
Programs
FAQ
Contact Us

A Better Life for Older Americans

Welcome to eldersrus.cambridge.org. This site will ~~to~~ help you enjoy your later years. In the future, the world's population get older. By 2050, about 20 percent of the world's people would be 70 or older. Some people say an older society going to be a problem. At eldersrus.org, we disagree. We predict that older people help society. In the future, older people in workplaces will to help companies make better decisions. Certainly, tomorrow's older population going to need more health care. In the future, there will perhaps to be better health care for everyone of all ages. Active, healthy seniors can change the world. Click here to read more about eldersrus.cambridge.org. In the future, you will to be happy you did!

Self-Assessment

Circle the word or phrase that correctly completes each sentence.

1. _____ me take my grandfather to the doctor tomorrow?

   a. You will help b. Will you help c. Help will you

2. Where _____ in your old age?

   a. will you live b. you will live c. you live

3. Tom doesn't take care of his health. _____ to the age of 100.

   a. He isn't living b. He not live c. He won't live

4. As more older people retire, companies _____ enough workers.

   a. will not probably have b. will probably not have c. will have not probably

5. **A:** _____ at Sofia's retirement party? **B:** No, he probably won't.

   a. Will Diego being b. Where will Diego be c. Will Diego be

6. **A:** What will he do after he retires? **B:** _____ another job or maybe travel somewhere.

   a. He will possibly get b. He probably gets c. He will certainly get

7. _____ a lot of money for a happy retirement.

   a. I going to save b. I'm going to save c. I'm going save

8. A better Social Security system will take a lot of time. _____ it immediately.

   a. We're not fix b. We not fixing c. We're not going to fix

9. Sorry, but I can't talk now. I'm in a meeting. _____ when it's over.

   a. I'm going call you b. I'll call you c. I call you

10. The number of Bottley College students over 70 _____ in the future.

    a. will increase b. is increasing c. increase

11. After retirement, I'm going to move to Florida. Where _____ after retirement?

    a. are you going to live b. you are going to live c. are you living

12. I don't know everything about the future, but I'm sure the population _____ older.

    a. will possibly get b. will perhaps get c. will undoubtedly get

13. In the future, driving will probably be easier for older people. Satellites and computers _____ cars.

    a. are probably controlling b. will probably control c. probably control

14. In 20 years, maybe doctors ____ patients through the Internet.

    a. will take care of   b. would take care of   c. take care of

15. Movies in the future ____ more parts for older actors.

    a. will to have   b. will have   c. will

UNIT 18

Future Time Clauses and Future Conditionals

Learning to Communicate

Future Time Clauses

1 Read the paragraph about dictionaries. Underline eight more future time clauses.

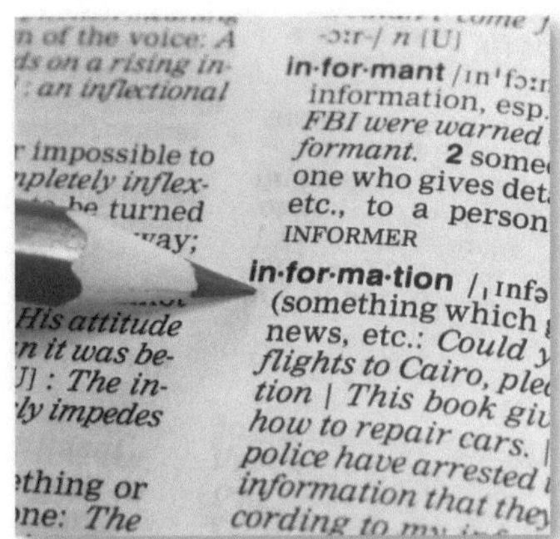

Once a word becomes popular, people will expect a dictionary to include it. However, not every word is good enough for the dictionary. A word will pass many tests before it gets into the dictionary. For example, here is how one well-known dictionary normally adds new words. After the editors see a new word, they will put it on a list of interesting words. The editor will make a note about the word as soon as it appears anywhere. What does it mean? Who is using it? Where do people use the word? Usually, until the editors have hundreds of notes for the word, they will not think about it very much. When they have a large number of notes, the editors will make a special card for the word. When the company plans a new dictionary, a person called the head reader will review all the information from the editors. After the head reader considers thousands of words, he or she will choose the best words. Then the company's managers will discuss those choices. As soon as the managers name the lucky new words, writers will write definitions for them. Finally, we will find them in the dictionary.

2 Write sentences about how Gabriel and Julia will teach their infant Ana English and Portuguese at home. Use the time words in parentheses.

1. Ana / be / one year old — Gabriel and Julia / sing English and Portuguese children's songs to her

   (before) *Before Ana is one year old, Gabriel and Julia will sing English and Portuguese children's songs to her.*

2. Ana / start to speak — Gabriel and Julia / teach her the names of things in Portuguese and English

   (as soon as) ____

3. Gabriel / talk to Ana — he / only use English

   (when) ____

4. Ana / seem to understand — Gabriel / repeat words in English

   (until) ____

5. Ana / go to bed — Julia / read her a story in Portuguese

   (before) ____

6. Ana / be / four years old — Julia / find day-care with Portuguese and English speakers

   (once) ____

Future Conditionals; Questions with Time Clauses and Conditional Clauses

1 **A** Read the radio report about a special dog. Complete the sentences with the correct forms of the verbs in parentheses.

Announcer: Now, here's a special feature on dog training by Nadia Flint. If you __have__ (1) (have) a dog, you __will like__ (2) (like) this.

Nadia: If you ____________ (3) (want) to teach your dog some words, you ____________ (4) probably ____________ (4) (teach) him with actions. If you ____________ (5) (want) to teach him the command "sit," you ____________ (6) (push) his back legs down and say "sit." However, if your dog ____________ (7) (be) like Bobby the border collie, you and he ____________ (8) (share) a much larger vocabulary. Dr. Erin Brown is Bobby's trainer. Welcome, Dr. Brown.

Dr. Brown: Thank you, Nadia.

Nadia: So, Dr. Brown, how many words does Bobby know?

Dr. Brown: He knows more than 300 words. If you ____________ (9) (take) a high school German class, you ____________ (10) (learn) less than that in a whole semester. If we ____________ (11) (show) him an object such as a book and say "book," he ____________ (12) (remember) the word later. He will go and pick up a book.

Nadia: OK, so if Bobby ____________ (13) (see) a thing and ____________ (14) (hear) a word, ____________ (15) he always ____________ (15) (learn) its name?

Dr. Brown: Not always, but usually. Oh, and listen to this. This is amazing! If I ____________ (16) (put) a familiar toy and a new toy in front of him and say the new toy's name, he ____________ (17) (choose) the new toy.

Nadia: Really? That's fascinating! Thank you, Dr. Brown. I'm sure that if our listeners ____________ (18) (have) dogs, they ____________ (19) (try) to teach them some new words right after this report!

B Write *Yes / No* future conditional questions and questions with time clauses. Use the answers to help you.

1. **A:** I know you will soon get a dog. *If you use actions, will your dog learn to sit?*

   B: Yes. If I use actions, my dog will learn to sit.

2. **A:** ______________________________

   B: Yes. If my dog is like Bobby, I will teach new words to him.

3. **A:** ______________________________

   B: Yes. When Dr. Brown teaches Bobby a word, she will say the word.

4. **A:** ______________________________

   B: Yes. She will show him a thing if she wants him to learn the word.

5. **A:** ______________________________

   B: Yes. If Bobby learns a word now, he will remember it later.

6. **A:** ______________________________

   B: Yes. Bobby will learn a word once he hears it.

7. **A:** ______________________________

   B: Yes. If listeners have dogs, they will try to teach them new words.

Avoid Common Mistakes

1 Circle the mistakes.

1. If Laila goes to India, **she will speak** (a) Hindi. If Tom **will go** (b) to India, he will use English. If I **go** (c) to India, I'll study a new language.
2. When Ivan **finishes** (a) college, he will get a job. **After** (b) Jim finishes his Malay class, he will get a job in Malaysia. Before I **will go** (c) to Japan, I will get a job there.
3. When I get married, **I have** (a) children. **When** (b) I have children, I will teach them Chinese. When I **have** (c) children, I'll take them to visit China.

4. When I **will write** (a) English, I'll use the English alphabet. When I **write** (b) Russian, I'll use Cyrillic. When I write Arabic, **I'll use** (c) Arabic script.
5. I'm sure I'll become a rock star. **If** (a) I **become** (b) a rock star, **I'll get** (c) famous.
6. If I **do** (a) well in school, I will become a lawyer. If I **will be** (b) a lawyer, I **will help** (c) the poor.
7. If I **train** (a) my dog well, he **will understand** (b) many words. **When** (c) I am patient, he will learn the names of things.
8. When cats **hear** (a) their names often, they will easily learn them. When apes **watch** (b) trainers, they will learn signs. When dogs **will hear** (c) words, they will learn them.

2 Find and correct the mistakes in the article about a parrot.

Birds Do More Than Copy

If some birds will be well trained, they will speak. If Gus, a parrot, will hear you say "hi," he will say "hi." Brian Green of Western University says, "If Gus will see a new thing, he will make up new words for it. Yesterday, Gus saw a plum and called it 'cherry apple.' In the future, if I show him something similar to what he knows, I listen for Gus's new name for it." If most parrots will hear a name, they will repeat it. Gus does more. As soon as Gus will hear a new person's name, he will make a sentence, like "Hi, Susan." When Gus continues to talk so well, he changes the way we think about bird communication.

Self-Assessment

Circle the word or phrase that correctly completes each sentence.

1. When I _____ this phone call, I will talk to you.

   a. will finish b. finish c. am finishing

2. Usually _____ a child starts school, he or she will learn to talk.

   a. before b. after c. when

3. Until I learn the Bambara language, I _____ French to communicate with people in Mali.

   a. using   b. use   c. will use

4. If he calls the main office, he will _____ with Mr. Davis.

   a. speaks   b. speak   c. to speak

5. Will _____ new sounds if you study Chinese?

   a. learn you   b. you learn   c. learn

6. What _____ if you speak with the president of the college?

   a. will you say   b. will say   c. you will say

7. **A:** If I send Megumi an e-mail, _____ ? **B:** Yes, she will.

   a. she will answer   b. will she answer   c. does she answer

8. If I _____ in a dictionary, will I find the word *e-mail*?

   a. to look   b. will look   c. look

9. If Native Americans use their languages in daily speech, the languages _____ .

   a. survive   b. will survive   c. surviving

10. When Rodrigo _____ a new dog, he will train it to understand a lot of words.

    a. gets   b. will get   c. will he get

11. Once you finish your college program, what _____ ?

    a. you will do   b. do you will   c. will you do

12. Where will you go once _____ a new language?

    a. you will learn   b. you learn   c. learn

13. If we go upstairs really late tonight, we _____ quietly. The children are sleeping.

    a. will speak   b. speak   c. are speaking

14. After I _____ enough money, I will go to China to study Chinese.

    a. will save   b. am saving   c. save

15. If I learn Arabic writing, I _____ the language better.

    a. speak   b. will speak   c. do speak

UNIT 19

Ability

Amazing Science

Ability with *Can* and *Could*

1 Complete the sentences about storms. Use *can* or *can't* and the verbs in parentheses.

1. A storm *can cause* (cause) a lot of damage.
2. When people don't know that a storm is coming, they ________________ (prepare) for it.
3. With new technology, scientists ________________ (make) better weather predictions.
4. Satellites[1] ________________ (take) pictures that show exactly where a storm is.
5. Scientists ________________ (learn) everything from satellites. They also use other technological tools.
6. New kinds of airplanes ________________ (fly) into a storm and learn more.
7. These "drone" airplanes fly into dangerous storms where people ________________ (go).
8. There are no people inside. The drones ________________ (fly) without a pilot.
9. Computers ________________ (analyze) information from satellites and drones.
10. Through computer networks, scientists around the world ________________ (share) weather information with each other and tell weather forecasters.
11. Weather forecasters ________________ (give) people instructions about how to be safe in a storm.
12. Scientists ________________ (stop) storms, but they can warn people about them.

[1] **satellite:** a complex machine in space that can take pictures of Earth, help with communications, etc.

2 Complete the sentences about roads. Circle the correct word.

1. Roads today **can / could** do amazing things.
2. In the past, many roads **can't / couldn't** last very long.
3. In the twentieth century, heavy traffic and bad weather **can / could** damage roads.
4. However, now scientists **can / could** make new, long-lasting roads.
5. These new roads **can / could** last a long time without repairs.
6. In the past, engineers **can't / couldn't** make roads that were environmentally friendly.
7. Now we have roads that **can / could** protect the environment.
8. For example, a new road in Italy **can / could** "eat" pollution and clean the air.
9. In the United States, we **can / could** build roads that collect heat from sunshine. The heat keeps buildings warm.
10. We **can / could** also build new roads out of recycled materials.
11. About 100 years ago, drivers **can't / couldn't** imagine these changes were possible.

3 A What technology can you use? Write sentences that are true for you. Use *can* or *can't* and the words in parentheses.

1. (Internet / surf) *I can surf the Internet.*
2. (smartphone / use) I can use a smartphone.
3. (GPS navigator / understand) I can understand a GPS navigator.
4. (video chat calls / make) I can make video chat calls.

B In the past, could you use the technology in A? Write sentences that are true for you. Use *could* or *couldn't* and the time in parentheses.

1. (as a child) *I couldn't surf the Internet as a child.*
2. (ten years ago) I couldn't make video calls 10 years ago.
3. (five years ago) I could understand a GPS navigator 5 years ago.
4. (last year) I could use a smart phone last year.

4 Read the blog about weather. Write answers to the questions. Use *can, can't, could,* or *couldn't.*

BLOG SEARCH

Cory's Weather Page - June 1

Spring Weather in History

- In June 1957, 416 people died in Hurricane Audrey. Scientists did not use satellites for forecasting the weather. There were no satellites for scientists. There were some storm warnings on TV, but many people did not have TVs.
- On June 10, 2008, there was a snowstorm in northern Minnesota. A lot of people did not go to work or school because of the weather. Snow in June in the United States? Many people in Minnesota thought it was impossible. Wrong!

Today and Beyond

There are no clouds in the satellite pictures. Look out your window. There is a lot of sunshine today, and there is no chance of rain today. This is a great day to walk, ride your bike, or work in your garden. You won't see the sun tomorrow, however. You will only see rain.

1. Why was Hurricane Audrey a surprise to scientists?
   they / use / satellites to watch the storm
   They couldn't use satellites to watch the storm.
2. What happened because many people in 1957 had no TV or radio?
   storm warnings / reach them
   The storm warnings couldn't reach them.
3. What did many people in Minnesota think about a snowstorm in the spring?
   they thought that / it / happen
   People thought it couldn't be possible.
4. Was it possible for everyone to go to work or school?
   no / a lot of people / go / to work or school
   No, a lot of people couldn't go to work or school.
5. How does Cory know that today will be clear?
   he / see / any clouds in the satellite pictures
   He can't see ...
6. Is this a good day for riding bikes?
   yes / people / ride their bikes today
   Yes people can ride ...
7. What weather can Cory predict for tomorrow?
   he / predict / rain / for tomorrow
   He can predict ...

Be Able To

1 Rewrite the sentences about inventions. Use *be able to* with the verbs in bold from the previous sentences.

1. DARPA is a U.S. government research group. It **can invent** some amazing things.

   DARPA _is able to invent_ some amazing things.

2. DARPA invented a computer network that **could reach** all around the world.

   DARPA invented a computer network that was able to reach all around the world.

3. Now you **can use** this network. We call it the Internet.

   Now you are able to use this network.

4. At first, only the military used GPS. By 1993, many people **could use** the system.

   By 1993, many people were able to use the system.

5. DARPA also invented airplanes that radar **couldn't see.**

   DARPA also invented airplanes that radar wasn't able to see.

6. These "stealth" planes **can fly** into dangerous places where other planes **can't go.**

   "Stealth" planes are able to fly where other planes aren't able to go.

7. Most people believe that DARPA **can make** more amazing inventions.

   Most people think DARPA is able to make more inventions.

2 A Read the paragraphs about a TV show called *The Jetsons.* Circle the word or phrase that correctly completes each question.

The Jetsons is a TV cartoon show from the 1960s. It's still on cable TV, so even young people know about it. When new technology comes out, sometimes people say, "That's like *The Jetsons*."

The show is about a family in the future. The Jetson family does not clean their house. Rosie the robot does all the housework. When they want food, they press a button on a machine and a meal appears. When he dresses for work, George Jetson stands in a machine. The machine puts on his clothes.

In the Jetsons' world, people have cars that fly. Also, people can fly with jetpacks – backpacks that have rockets. They can take vacations on the moon. They also stay in hotels that float in space.

1. _____ see *The Jetsons* on TV now?

   a. People are able to b. Are people able to

2. _____ keep their house clean?

   a. How the Jetsons are able to b. How are the Jetsons able to

3. _____ get food when they press a button?

   a. The Jetsons able to b. Are the Jetsons able to

4. _____ dress for work?

   a. How is George Jetson able to b. How George Jetson is able to

5. _____ fly?

   a. How are the Jetsons able to b. How the Jetsons are able to

6. _____ take vacations?

   a. Where are people able to b. Where people able to

B Write answers to the questions in A with *be able to.*

1. Yes, people are able to see the Jetsons on TV now.
2. ______________________________

____

3. ____

____

4. ____

____

5. ____

____

6. ____

____

Avoid Common Mistakes

1 Circle the mistakes.

1. Kevin **can't** (a) make new inventions. He **not able to** (b) get enough money. He **isn't able to** (c) buy things he needs.
2. Doctors finally **able to** (a) make a "smart pill." They **were able to** (b) test it. **Were they able to** (c) sell it?
3. DARPA **was able to** (a) invent the Internet. It **was able to** (b) make stealth planes. It **was able** (c) develop GPS.
4. **I'm not able to** (a) use this GPS. I **can not** (b) use that one, either. I **can't** (c) understand these things.
5. You **able to** (a) see this machine? **Can** (b) you tell me what it is? **Are you able to** (c) use it?
6. Computers **can** (a) help scientists. Computers, however, **can't** (b) think. Only people **able to** (c) design inventions.
7. Einstein **was able to** (a) do mathematics. He **wasn't able to** (b) use computers. In 1905, he finally **could** (c) develop a new theory.
8. When **will the city able to** (a) recover from the storm? How **will the people be able to** (b) rebuild? Who **can** (c) help the people?

2 Find and correct seven more mistakes in the paragraph about inventing.

A Famous Scientist Talks About Inventing

In my high school, we were not able do experiments. We did not have a lab. I was sad, because you can not become an inventor without a lab. My parents told me to build my own lab in our garage, so I did. I could build a pretty good one. Now, at City College, I able to use one of the best labs in the world. When I have an idea for an invention, I am able build it. Here's my advice to young people: Go to a school where you able to use a good lab. Computers are good, but you can not really invent things with them alone. Remember: A good inventor is able use his or her hands.

Self-Assessment

Circle the word or phrase that correctly completes each sentence.

1. I'm sorry, but I _____ you with your science homework now. I'm too busy.

   a. can help b. can't help c. couldn't help

2. In the future, _____ tell their wheelchairs where to go?

   a. people be able to b. people will be able to c. will people be able to

3. Where _____ find a medical expert?

   a. can b. we can c. can we

4. Some colleges _____ hire famous scientists to teach classes.

   a. able to b. are able to c. are able

5. _____ computers able to invent things?

   a. Is b. Can c. Are

6. After you become a doctor, _____ invent a pill to make people smart?

   a. will you can b. will you be able to c. you will be able to

7. In 1960, NASA _____ send the first weather satellite into space.

   a. could to b. able to c. was able to

8. Where _____ a room with WiFi?

   a. can we find b. we can find c. we find can

9. My friends _____ go to the Science Museum.

   a. wasn't able to (b.) weren't able to c. am not able to

10. _____ people with rocket-powered arms _____ lift heavy objects?

   (a.) Are . . . able to b. Able . . . to c. Able to . . . are

11. Pavel is going to _____ make a lot of money from his inventions someday.

   a. able to b. is able to (c.) be able to

12. The government wants to _____ inventions that help the economy.

   (a.) be able to find b. can find c. is able to find

13. In a few years, cars _____ go for hundreds of miles on electric power.

   a. are be able to (b.) will be able to c. going to able to

14. Some scientists _____ make any money from their inventions.

   a. cannot to b. could not to (c.) are not able to

15. _____ doctors _____ bring us amazing medical inventions over the next ten years?

   (a.) Will . . . be able to b. Are . . . will be able to c. Able . . . to bring

UNIT 20

Requests and Offers

Good Causes

Permission

1 Read the e-mails about a volunteer project. Underline the expressions in Feyza Entep's e-mail that request permission. Circle the expressions in Dr. John Lance's e-mail that answer the requests.

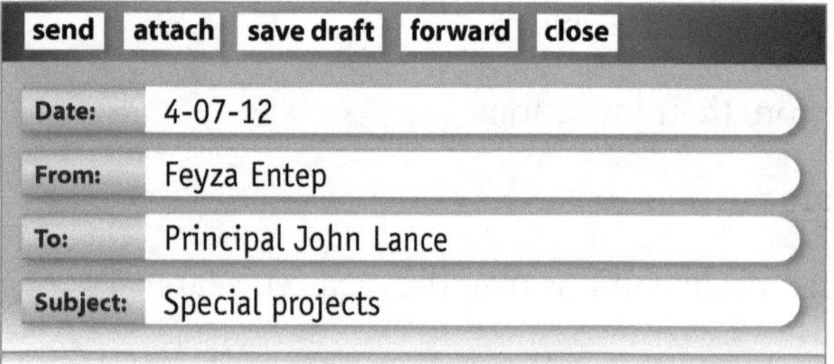

send | attach | save draft | forward | close

Date: 4-07-12
From: Feyza Entep
To: Principal John Lance
Subject: Special projects

Dear Dr. Lance,

As you know, I'm the president of the Student Service Club. I'm writing to ask your permission to organize some activities in our community. Every year, we have made a holiday dinner for homeless people. Can we do that again? May I contact the newspaper about this? They might write an article about it. Also, do you mind if we have a 3-mile race to raise money for our projects? Finally, could we use the school parking lot in May for our car wash? It raises money to send kids to summer camp. Thanks for your time.

Feyza Entep

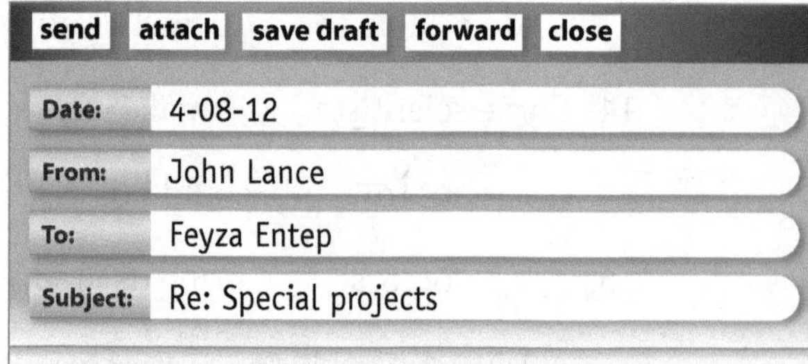

send | attach | save draft | forward | close

Date: 4-08-12
From: John Lance
To: Feyza Entep
Subject: Re: Special projects

Dear Feyza,

Thank you for your e-mail. I'm glad that our Service Club is so active. About the holiday dinner: Sure. No problem. Sorry, but please don't tell the newspaper about it. We can serve only about 100 people. I'm afraid I don't like the idea of the race. If someone gets hurt, we might get in trouble. You can certainly do the car wash. We do this every year, right? I think it's a great activity.

Dr. John Lance

2 Complete the conversation. Circle the correct words or phrases.

Heather: I hear you're starting your volunteer job at an animal shelter today. **Could I / May** (1) go with you?

Quin: OK, but my car is not running well. **Can please / Do you mind if** (2) we take your car?

Heather: **Not at all. / Yes.** (3) How do we get there?

Quin: I'm not sure. **Can / Do you mind** (4) I borrow your map?

Heather: No problem. Oh, sorry. This is the wrong map.

Quin: Oh. **Can please I / Can I please** (5) use your cell phone?

Heather: OK, but **could I / do you mind if** (6) ask why?

Quin: I'll call and ask for directions. **Can I / Do you mind if** (7) borrow a pen?

Heather: **Sure. No problem. / Not at all.** (8)

3 Write responses to the questions about the volunteer projects. Use the information in parentheses to help you choose a positive or negative response. Sometimes more than one answer is possible.

1. Could you please tell me the name of your organization?

   (yes) *Certainly. We're the Newtown Aid Group.*

2. Can you tell me how to spell "Newtown"?

   (yes) ______

3. I heard that your organization gives people free lunches. Can I have one?

   (no) ______

4. Do you mind if I help with some of your projects?

   (yes) ______

5. I don't have a car. Could I ride with you?

   (no) ______

6. I'm only 16 years old. May I join your organization?

   (no) ______

7. Could I work on a volunteer project?

   (yes) ______

8. Thanks. Do you mind if I ask you more questions later?

   (yes) ______

Requests and Offers

1 Complete the conversation between Ken (a student) and Mr. Cook (a teacher). Circle the more formal requests and answers.

Ken: Hi Mr. Cook. **Could / Can** (1) you answer some questions for me?

Mr. Cook: Hi, Ken. **Yes. Of course. / Sure, no problem.** (2) Come in. **Can / Would** (3) you close the door?

Ken: **Sure, no problem. / Certainly.** (4)

Mr. Cook: What questions do you have?

Ken: Well, I feel bad because I don't do any volunteering. **Will / Would** (5) you be able to give me some advice?

Mr. Cook: I'll try. **Could / Will** (6) you please tell me what you want to do?

Ken: I'm not sure. Help poor people, maybe.

Mr. Cook: Why don't you volunteer at a homeless organization?

Ken: OK. **Could / Will** (7) you call an organization for me and find me a volunteer job?

Mr. Cook: **I'm sorry / No** (8), Ken. You have to do this yourself. I can't find a volunteer job for you.

2 Complete the conversations about volunteering. Circle the correct words and phrases.

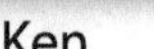

Ken

Karen

Brian

Ken: Hi, **could / may** (1) you help me? I want to speak to the manager.

Karen: **I'm sorry / Sure** (2), our manager isn't here right now. **I'll / I may** (3) connect you with her assistant instead.

Ken: **That would be great / I'm afraid not**.
(4)

Brian: Hello. Marcia Dean's office. Brian speaking.

Ken: Hi. I'm interested in volunteering. **Could / Couldn't** you tell me what opportunities
(5)
you have?

Brian: **Certainly / Please**. We always need people to help serve food to the homeless.
(6)
Could you do that?

Ken: Yes, I **could / can**.
(7)

Brian: OK, if you really want to help, **may / would** you please give me your
(8)
e-mail address?

3 Janet volunteers to do art projects with children. Read the conversation between Janet and her manager. Write Janet's offers to help. Then use your own ideas to write the manager's responses.

1. **Manager:** We need people to bring some paper and crayons.

   Janet: *I'll bring some paper and crayons on Tuesday.* (I'll / Tuesday)

   Manager: *That would be great!*

2. **Manager:** We need people to drive the children to the art center.

   Janet: ______________________ (Can I / after school)

   Manager: ______________________

3. **Manager:** We need a volunteer who will explain the project.

   Janet: ______________________ (May I / to the children)

   Manager: ______________________

4. **Manager:** We need two volunteers to clean the tables after the class.

   Janet: ______________________ (I can / with Dan)

   Manager: ______________________

5. **Manager:** We need someone to get more volunteers.

   Janet: ______________________ (I could / at my college)

   Manager: ______________________

Avoid Common Mistakes

1 Circle the mistakes.

1. John, **could you lift** (a) this box? Yanping, **could you to help** (b)? Kyle, **could you open** (c) the door?
2. Can you help me, **please** (a)? Can **please** (b) you call the shelter? Can you **please** (c) tell them I'm sick?
3. **A:** Could I visit the animal shelter? **B:** Yes, **you could** (a). **A:** Could I volunteer there? **B:** Yes, **you can** (b).
   A: Could I bring friends with me? **B:** No, **you can't** (c).
4. **A:** Would you help me train volunteers? **B:** **Sure, I'll do that** (a). **A:** Would you put out chairs for the volunteers? **B:** **Sure, I would** (b). **A:** Would you e-mail the volunteers? **B:** **Sure, I will** (c).
5. Excuse me, sir. **May I ask** (a) you for help? **Could I ask** (b) you for help? **May I to ask** (c) for help?
6. Could I **please** (a) leave a message? Could I talk to a volunteer, **please** (b)? Could **please** (c) they call me back?
7. **A:** Could you give me a ride to the shelter? **B:** **Sorry, I can't** (a). **A:** Could you give me directions?
   B: **Yes, I could** (b). **A:** Could you show me a map? **B:** **Yes, I can** (c).
8. **A:** Would you cook the vegetables? **B:** **Yes, I would** (a). **A:** Would you pass me a spoon? **B:** **Yes, I will** (b).
   A: Would you cook dinner tomorrow? **B:** **No. I don't have time** (c).

2 Find and correct the mistakes in the memo about a charity car wash.

From: The Management Team

Re: Organizing Saturday's Car Wash

This Saturday, we'll have our office's charity car wash. Can you ~~to~~ help? Could please we share the work? Could our marketing department to bring towels? We need buckets to carry water. Will the salespeople to bring some? Advertising department, can you direct please cars into the car wash? We need lots of help. Would you to ask your family and friends to help? The technology team said, "Yes, we would." Thanks in advance. People have asked, "Could please the managers bring pizza?" Yes, we could!

Self-Assessment

Circle the word or phrase that correctly completes each sentence.

1. _____ go with you to the meeting?

   a. I could   b. Could I   c. Can

2. My phone's not working. _____ if I use yours?

   a. Do you mind b. You mind c. Do I mind

3. **A:** Could I stay at your house tonight? **B:** No, _____ . We already have guests.

   a. could b. you couldn't c. you can't

4. Excuse me. _____ ask for your opinion about the project?

   a. I may b. May I c. May you

5. Can I _____ with your volunteer group?

   a. to work b. working c. work

6. **A:** Could I use your car? **B:** _____ . I don't let anyone use it.

   a. Sorry b. Sure c. Afraid

7. **A:** _____ ask you a question? **B:** No, not at all.

   a. Can I b. Could I c. Do you mind if I

8. **A:** Could you bring some pizza? **B:** Sure, _____ .

   a. no problem b. I'm afraid not c. not at all

9. _____ these boxes in your car?

   a. Can please I put b. Can I please put c. Can I put please

10. _____ bring a salad. Could you bring some bread?

    a. I would b. I'll c. Will

11. **A:** I can help you carry those boxes. **B:** _____ .

    a. No b. No, thanks c. No, I can't

12. _____ please explain your organization to me?

    a. Would you b. Would c. You

13. **A:** _____ help you clean up after the dinner. **B:** That would be great.

    a. I'll b. I would c. I may

14. **A:** Could I work with you on the assignment? **B:** _____ .

    a. Not at all b. I'm afraid c. That would be great

15. **A:** Can I give you a call about the volunteer job later tonight? **B:** _____ .

    a. Sure, you could b. Sure, you can c. Sure, you will

UNIT

21 Advice and Suggestions

The Right Job

Advice

1 Complete the statements about jobs in the future. Use the verbs in parentheses with *should, shouldn't, ought to,* and *had better.* Sometimes more than one answer is possible.

1. Schools *should prepare* OR *ought to prepare* (prepare) students for jobs that will be popular in the future.
2. Training programs ______________ (not / train) students for jobs that computers could do, or those students may not get a job in the future.
3. Students ______________ (ask) their advisers to help them assess their skills.
4. Every student ______________ (do) research and find out where the jobs will be in the future.
5. A smart student ______________ (think) about jobs that are in the environmental and health-care industries.
6. **A:** Why __________ he or she __________ (think) about jobs in those industries? **B:** Because job experts say that those industries will grow.
7. Students ______________ (not worry) about too few jobs as electricians, hairstylists, and dental hygienists because they will still be good choices.
8. **A:** __________ they __________ (be) concerned about their future? **B:** Yes, but they are doing the right thing by being in school.
9. Students ______________ (make) careful decisions now, or they will regret their choices later.

2 Complete the conversations. Use the words in parentheses with *should.*

Conversation 1

Daniella: Joseph, you've been very stressed lately. Is it because of your job?

Joseph: Yeah. I'm thinking about quitting. What should I do (1) (I / what / do)?

Daniella: Well, you shouldn't quit before you've found another job.

Joseph: So, should I start (2) (I / start) looking for a new job?

Daniella: Yes, you should.

Joseph: ____________ (3) (I / look / where)?

Daniella: You could go to an employment agency.

Joseph: Thanks, Daniella. You have really good advice. Just one more thing, could you read my résumé before I send it in?

Daniella: Of course! ____________ (4) (come / I) by tomorrow?

Joseph: Sure. Tomorrow is good.

Daniella: OK. See you tomorrow!

Conversation 2

Ivan: Hi, Emily. How are you?

Emily: Hi, Ivan. I'm good. My son is coming home next week for summer vacation. I'm excited to see him.

Ivan: That's nice. Does he have any plans?

Emily: I don't think so. I'm worried he'll be bored. ____________ (5) (he / get) a job?

Ivan: He should! It will keep him busy. My company is hiring summer interns. He could apply here.

Emily: That's a good idea! ____________ (6) (send / who / he) his résumé to?

Ivan: He can e-mail it to me. I'll give it to the human resources department.

Emily: And ____________ (7) (when / e-mail / he) it to you?

Ivan: The application deadline is next Monday.

Emily: Thanks, Ivan!

3 Read the sentences about Manuel and his wife. Complete the advice with the words in parentheses and the phrases in the box.

buy a house now	~~go to an employment agency~~
call the company to find out how to apply	listen to him and help him
find some interviewing tips on the Internet	post his résumé online
get some job training	quit until he gets a new job

1. Manuel wants a new job. He is not sure what he should do

   (ought to) He *ought to go to an employment agency*.

2. He wants to quit his job right now.

   (not / had better) He ______.

3. He wants a lot of employers to see his résumé.

   (should) He ______.

4. He sees an interesting job online with a company.

   (should) He ______.

5. His wife doesn't want him to change jobs. She doesn't listen to him when he talks about it.

   (ought to) She ______.

6. He needs more skills to get a better-paying job.

   (should) He ______.

7. He is very nervous about going to interviews.

   (ought to) He ______.

8. He and his wife want to buy a house, but they aren't saving much money.

   (not / should) They ______.

4 Rewrite the imperatives as statements of advice. Use *should*, *ought to*, or *had better*. Some sentences are negative. Sometimes more than one answer is possible.

1. Decide what job you want.

   You should decide what job you want.

2. Focus on jobs that require your special skills.

   ______

3. Don't waste time on jobs that don't sound interesting.

   ______

4. Be sure that you have a good résumé, or you may not attract good companies.

____

5. Find out about free or low-cost training programs.

____

6. Tell everyone you know that you are looking for a job.

____

7. Don't put untrue statements on your résumé, or you may get into trouble later.

____

Suggestions

1 Complete the conversation about choosing a career as a medical assistant. Circle the correct words or phrases.

A: I think I want to be a medical assistant.

B: Great. Maybe **you could / could you** (1) work in one of the clinics in our neighborhood.

A: Yes, I'd like to, but I'm not sure I have the time to study and work at the same time.

B: **You might want to / Why not** (2) find out about services for students like you.

A: Yes, I should. I know I'll need support.

B: **Why not / Why don't** (3) talk to a medical assistant and find out how he or she did it?

A: That's a great idea. Maybe I'll stop by the clinic down the street today.

B: Yeah. **You might want to / Why not** (4) call them first and arrange an appointment.

A: OK, I will. **I could / Why don't I** (5) call them now?

B: Sure. I would tell them that your interview will be short.

A: How much time do you think I'll need?

B: You **might not want to / could** (6) schedule more than about 20 minutes. That place is always very busy.

2 Look at the checklist for job interviews. Complete the conversations with the words in the boxes. Use the information from the checklist.

Are You Ready?
A Checklist for Job Interviews

Appearance

Hair
- ☐ cut
- ☐ washed
- ☐ brushed

Clothes
- ☐ clean
- ☐ in style for business

Fingernails
- ☐ cut
- ☐ clean

Personal matters
- ☐ fresh breath
- ☐ not too much perfume / cologne[1]

Behavior

Smiles
- ☐ friendly
- ☐ not too big

Conversation
- ☐ pleasant
- ☐ ask the employer questions
- ☐ no topics that cause disagreements

---

[1]**perfume** and **cologne:** liquids that make a person's body smell nice

Conversation 1

you might not	~~why don't~~	why don't

A: I'm going to a job interview. I hope I look OK.

B: Sure, you look fine. Maybe your hair is a little long, though. *Why don't* (1) you get a haircut?

A: I don't have time to get a haircut. My interview is this afternoon. Do you like my new clothes? I'm going to wear them to the interview.

B: They're nice, but ________ (2) want to wear bright colors. That red jacket looks too informal.

A: Bright colors are popular this year.

B: OK, but ________ (3) you wear less perfume? It smells a little too strong.

Conversation 2

why don't you	you could	you might not

A: How should I smile? I don't want to look bad.

B: ________________ (4) practice smiles in the mirror. You don't want to have a smile that's too big.

A: Right. I should also practice conversations.

B: Yes. Be natural, but ________________ (5) want to talk about topics that cause disagreements.

A: I know what we can do! ________________ (6) practice a conversation with me? You can help me.

Avoid Common Mistakes

1 Circle the mistakes.

1. He**'d better think** (a) about his career. He **better take** (b) challenging projects. He **had better build** (c) some skills.
2. Companies **had better not lie** (a) in job ads. They **had better not break** (b) the law. They **had better not use** (c) silly ads.
3. You **could not wear** (a) those shoes to the interview. You **might not want to wear** (b) sports shoes. You **might not want to wear** (c) a T-shirt.
4. **Why not get** (a) a haircut? **Why not look** (b) your best? **Why not getting** (c) a different hairstyle?
5. You **might not want to use** (a) an interviewer's first name. You **could not be** (b) too informal. **You might not want to act** (c) too friendly.
6. **Why not to ask** (a) for a good salary? **Why not ask** (b) for money? **Why not get** (c) what you need?
7. Tim **better hurry** (a). He **had better be** (b) on time for the interview. He**'d better not be** (c) late.
8. **Why not get** (a) a part-time job? **Why not get** (b) some experience? **Why not earning** (c) some money?

2 Find and correct eight more mistakes in the web article about job hunting.

Job Hunting

The Best Advice for Job Hunters

When you look for a job, you had better be prepared. Here are five things to think about. First, why not thinking about what you do best? You should get a job that lets you do that. Next, ask yourself, "Can I be happy with this company?" If the answer is "no," you better not take a job there. Third, you better tell interviewers the truth. You had better not lie in a job interview, or you might lose your job later. Also, why not to act like a professional? You could not talk or dress the way you do with your friends. Pay close attention to your clothes. Why not to buy new clothes just for job interviews? Finally, you better stay positive, even if you do not get the job. There are other jobs out there. You had better look for one that is even better.

Self-Assessment

AW

Circle the word or phrase that correctly completes each sentence.

1. I ____ my job.

   a. should to quit (b.) ought to quit c. had better to quit

2. Someone who sleeps late ____ take a job that starts at 6:00 in the morning.

   (a.) had better not b. had not better c. better not

3. **A:** I don't have a good tie to wear for my interview. **B:** You ____ borrow one from me.

   a. better b. ought (c.) could

4. Tom ____ send a copy of his résumé to the company if he wants a job there.

   a. had (b.) had better c. better

5. When ____ call the company?

   a. an applicant should (b.) should an applicant c. should

6. Who _____ to schedule an interview?

   a. call should   b. call   (c.) should call

7. You _____ get advice from a career adviser.

   (a.) probably ought to   b. ought probably to   c. ought to probably

8. **A:** I'm not good at my job. **B:** Then you _____ find a different one.

   a. had better not   b. why not   (c.) had better

9. **A:** I can't find any job ads in the paper. **B:** You _____ search some websites.

   a. might to   b. might want   (c.) might want to

10. You _____ wear that baseball cap to the interview.

    a. might want to not   b. might not want   (c.) might not want to

11. Why _____ Ivan call the company for an interview?

    (a.) doesn't   b. not   c. don't

12. **A:** Is the college looking for any workers? **B:** I don't know. _____ them?

    a. Why not calling   b. Why not to call   (c.) Why not call

13. You forgot to tell the interviewer your e-mail address? _____ call and tell her.

    (a.) You'd better   b. You had   c. You better

14. That company does not pay very well. You _____ get a job there.

    a. might not to want   b. might to not want   (c.) might not want to

15. Why not _____ a job that will help build your career?

    a. to take   b. taking   (c.) take

1. b   6. c   11. a
2. a   7. a   12. c
3. c   8. c   13. a
4. b   9. c   14. c
5. b   10. c   15. c

UNIT 22

Necessity, Prohibition, and Preference

How to Sell It

Necessity and Prohibition

1 Complete the conversation about advertisements with the words in parentheses.

A: *Do* (1) businesses *have to talk* (1) (have to / talk) to every customer to sell their products?

B: That's not possible, so they ____________ (2) (must / spend) a lot of money on advertising their products everywhere. It can be very challenging.

A: What ____________ (3) they ____________ (3) (need to / do) to find the most customers?

B: They ____________ (4) (have to / advertise) their products on a lot of websites.

A: ____________ (5) companies ____________ (5) (need to / pay) a lot of money to advertise on websites?

B: No, they ____________ (6) (not / need to / pay) a lot of money. They can choose cheaper sites.

A: What ____________ (7) a company ____________ (7) (have to / look) for in a good website?

B: It ____________ (8) (have to / check) how much traffic[1] the site has.

A: What other things ____________ (9) a company ____________ (9) (need to / think) about when choosing websites?

B: It ____________ (10) (not / must / forget) that the website must also look appealing to consumers.

[1]**traffic:** the number of people who visit a website

2 Read the sentences about Adam's advertising business. Do the sentences say something is necessary, not necessary, or prohibited? Check (✓) the correct column.

	Necessary	Not Necessary	Prohibited
1. Companies that hire Adam don't have to plan their own advertising.		✓	
2. Adam has to learn about a company's products.			
3. Adam has to learn about a company's customers.			
4. Adam must convince customers to buy something.			
5. Adam must not lie in the ads.			
6. Adam doesn't have to make the ads himself. He hires other people to write them.			
7. Adam needs to tell other people what to write or draw.			
8. Adam must not forget to advertise his own company.			

3 Read the "Top Three Rules for Advertisers." Complete the statements with *have / has to, don't / doesn't have to,* or *must not.*

Top Three Rules for Advertisers

Understand what the customer likes.	Customers pay attention to what they like. Play the kind of music your customer likes. Talk about the things your customer wants.
Be positive.	Don't talk about the product's weaknesses. Tell how the product is better than other products and how it will help the customer.
Make your message short and easy to understand.	It is not necessary to have a long commercial. Short commercials can be effective, too.

1. An advertiser _must not_ forget who the customer is.
2. Advertisers ________________ use the customer's favorite things in ads.
3. A company ________________ use rock music in an ad if consumers don't like it.
4. An advertiser ________________ talk about a product's weaknesses.
5. A good ad ________________ concentrate on the good things about a product.
6. Advertisers ________________ have a commercial that is long.

Preference

1 Complete the conversations about television ads. Circle the correct word or phrase that correctly completes each sentence.

Conversation 1

Maria: ____ (1) watch old TV ads?

a. You would rather b. Would you rather c. You rather

Jun: I would prefer ____ (2) new ones. They're more creative.

a. to watch b. watch c. to watching

Maria: I disagree. New ads are not as clever. I ____ (3) watch old ones.

a. than b. 'd rather c. rather

Jun: Why ____ (4) see old ads? The technology was really simple.

a. rather would you b. you would rather c. would you rather

Maria: But the ideas were more clever. I ____ (5) this topic anymore.

a. 'd not rather discuss b. 'd rather not discuss c. rather not discuss

Conversation 2

Brad: The Super Bowl is on this Sunday. ____ (6) watch it for the football or for the ads?

a. You would rather b. Would you rather c. Rather would you

Gustavo: It's a football game! I ____ (7) it for the football.

a. 'd b. 'd like watch c. 'd like to watch

Brad: Some people ____ (8) the ads. Advertising companies save their best ads for the Super Bowl.

a. prefer watching b. prefer watch c. to watch

Gustavo: I ____ (9) watch ads for some products. I turn on the game to see a game!

a. 'd not rather b. 'd rather not c. rather not 'd

Brad: I understand. I like football, too, but I'd rather not ____ (10) a boring game.

a. to watch b. watching c. watch

2 Complete the article about ads and culture with the words in parentheses.

Many people *would prefer to think of* (1) (prefer / to / would / think of) ads as part of culture. Others ______________ (2) (prefer / to / would / study) how ads influence culture. I ______________ (3) ('d / give / like / to) two examples of how advertising really does influence culture.

Ads or Shows?

Most consumers say they ______________ (4) (not / watch / would / rather) ads on TV. However, some viewers really ______________ (5) (prefer / to / watch / would) the funny ads. One survey showed that 51 percent of people watching the Super Bowl ______________ (6) (rather / see / would) the ads than the game. The ads and the game are now both part of U.S. culture.

Music

Also, songs from ads can become part of a culture. Many ads contain music because customers ______________ (7) (hear / rather / would) music. One song from an ad in the 1970s, "I'd Like to Teach the World to Sing," became a Top Ten popular song. Many listeners ______________ (8) (listen / rather / would) to good ad songs ______________ (9) (listen / than) to most pop songs.

3 Complete the conversation with the words in parentheses.

A: ___Do___ (1) you ___prefer___ (1) (prefer) watching TV or using the Internet?

B: I like them both.

A: ________ (2) you ________ (2) (would rather) watch TV shows without ads?

B: Yes, I would, but most TV shows have ads.

A: What kinds of TV ads ________ (3) you ________ (3) (prefer)?

B: I prefer ads with good music and ads that are funny.

A: ________ (4) you ________ (4) (prefer) ads on the Internet or on TV?

B: Sometimes the ads on the Internet are annoying. I hate it when they pop up and you can't get rid of them.

A: Is there anything else you ____________ (5) (would like) to say?

B: I know websites need ads to make money, but I'd like the sites to have fewer of them.

HW

4 Answer the questions about your preferences. Write sentences that are true for you.

1. Would you rather buy products online or in a store? Why?

   I would rather buy products in a store because I like to see products before I buy them.

2. Would you like to work in an advertising company? Why or why not?

   ____

   ____

3. What are you going to do tonight? What would you prefer to do?

   ____

   ____

4. Do you prefer to text or call someone? Why?

   ____

   ____

Avoid Common Mistakes

1 Circle the mistakes.

1. This ad says lunch is free. Mehmet **doesn't have to** (a) pay for it. He **must not** (b) pay for it. He **doesn't have to** (c) eat it.
2. Kelly **would rather be** (a) an artist. She **would rather not study** (b) advertising. She **would rather to study** (c) art.
3. I **would like to write** (a) ads. I **would like work** (b) in New York. You **would prefer to work** (c) here.
4. John **rather not be** (a) a salesperson. He **would rather write** (b). He **would rather not sell** (c) things.
5. I **would prefer not to see** (a) Internet ads. I **would prefer to get** (b) news with no ads. I **would prefer see** (c) only the news.
6. You **don't need to show** (a) me the video today. I **must not see** (b) it right now. I **have to see** (c) it by Friday.
7. **Would you prefer to advertise** (a) in magazines? **Would you rather advertise** (b) on TV? **Would you rather to use** (c) the Internet?
8. Kelly **would rather get** (a) no ads in the mail. She **would rather not to read** (b) ads. She **would rather throw** (c) them away.

2 Find and correct seven more mistakes in the report about customers' opinions on advertisements.

Research Report Customer Opinions About Ads

We asked our customers what ads they ^would rather see. Most would rather to see ads that are funny. Many customers said ads must not be expensive. Ads don't have to have great art, they said. They would rather to see inexpensive ads with good jokes and good music. The music in an ad must not be famous. Customers prefer hear music that is happy and easy to sing instead of famous songs. About 60 percent of our customers rather see ads after a TV show than during the show. About 80 percent of them said they would rather not to see "pop-up" ads on the Internet – ads that come on the screen suddenly while you're looking at something else.

Self-Assessment

Circle the word or phrase that correctly completes each sentence.

1. Every student at Metro Community College _____ a $50 newspaper fee.

   a. has pay   b. must pay   c. must to pay

2. The student newspaper _____ money from ads, but it can't.

   a. would rather make   b. would to rather make   c. would rather to make

3. I want to e-mail Kelly, but I _____ her e-mail address.

   a. am need to get   b. need to get   c. need get

4. I _____ check the caller's name before I answer my phone. I'd rather not answer advertising calls.

   a. got   b. got to   c. 've got to

5. I heard you want to sell your car. _____ advertise it?

   a. Do you need to   b. You need to   c. Do you need

6. How much _____ pay to advertise it in the newspaper?

   a. you have to   b. do you have to   c. have to

7. _____ advertise online than advertise in newspapers?

   a. Would you rather   b. Would you prefer   c. Would you rather to

8. Where _____ see ads for clothes?

   a. would like to   b. would you to   c. would you like to

9. I think _____ see this commercial. It's really funny.

   a. you like to   b. you'd like to   c. you'll like to

10. I prefer _____ websites that don't have ads.

    a. go to   b. to go   c. to go to

11. Most people _____ get a lot of details about a product in an ad.

    a. would rather not   b. rather not   c. would not rather

12. Why _____ watch the ads than watch the football game?

    a. would you rather   b. rather would you   c. you would rather

13. _____ watch movies without any ads at the beginning?

    a. Would you prefer   b. Would you preferring   c. Would you prefer to

14. There are no ads at plays. I'd rather see a play than _____ a movie.

    a. to go to   b. go to   c. going to

15. **A:** Would you like to go to the mall? **B:** No, _____ .

    a. rather not   b. I rather   c. I'd rather not

UNIT

23 Present and Future Probability

Life Today, Life Tomorrow

Present Probability

1 Complete the sentences about Frank. Circle the correct modals.

1. Frank is a cook at a restaurant. He is looking for a new job.

   He **must / should** be unhappy with his current job.

2. Frank has worked at the restaurant for four years. He hasn't gotten a raise.

   He **might / couldn't** be unhappy because he thinks he deserves a raise.

3. The chef often tells Frank that he is doing a great job.

   The chef **can't / might not** be unhappy with Frank's work.

4. Other restaurant owners notice that Frank is very talented.

   Frank **must not / shouldn't** have a problem getting a new job.

5. Frank and his wife are expecting a baby in four months.

   They **can't / must** feel excited.

6. Frank and his wife are going to buy a new car next month.

   They **should / must not** have the new car before the baby comes.

7. Frank's wife isn't sure that he should change jobs right now.

   She **might not / shouldn't** think that it is a good thing to change jobs right now because of the baby.

8. Frank's wife hasn't been feeling well lately. Frank always keeps his cell phone near him and never goes out after work at night.

   He **must / could** be concerned about his wife.

2 Read the questions about a recent report on transportation. Complete the answers with *must* (*not*), *should*(*n't*), or *might* (*not*). Add *be* when necessary. Sometimes more than one answer is possible.

1. **A:** Is the scientists' report about transportation correct?

   B: It ___*must be*___. The scientists checked all the facts.

2. **A:** Are the scientists studying new kinds of cars?

   B: They ______________. They received money from the school for the research.

3. **A:** Do the scientists think electric cars are less harmful to the environment?

   B: Maybe. They ______________, but I didn't read all of the report.

4. **A:** I heard that some electric cars travel 600 miles with no stops.

   B: That ______________ be true. I know that no electric car can do that.

5. **A:** Is it possible for an average person to buy an electric car?

   B: It ______________. I'm fairly certain that they are very expensive.

6. **A:** Do most people know something about electric cars?

   B: They ______________. The news media often do stories about these cars.

7. **A:** Do electric cars affect people's health?

   B: They ______________. There could be negative effects. No one is really sure.

3 Complete the sentences about Susan. Use the words in parentheses and *must, must not, can't, might,* and *might not.* Sometimes more than one answer is possible.

1. Susan is studying to be an accountant. She works hard and does well on tests.

   She ___*must get good grades*___ (get / good grades).

2. Her parents never went to college. They tell everyone about their daughter.

   They ______________ (be / very proud of her).

3. Susan doesn't have classes on Wednesdays, but sometimes she goes to school and studies. It's Wednesday afternoon.

   She ______________ (be / at school).

4. Susan usually answers text messages. She isn't answering texts now.

   She ______________ (have / her phone on).

5. Her brother said that he wanted to quit his job. She knows that he loves his job.

   He ______________ (be / serious).

6. Her school is offering fewer classes this semester.

   It ______________ (have / enough money).

Modals of Future Probability

Classwork

1 Complete the statements about life in the future. Circle the correct modals.

1. Our jobs **won't / might not** be the same in the future. Everyone agrees that technology will change how we do our jobs.
2. Current technology has created many new professional jobs. Technology of the future **will / may** create new jobs, too. We are sure of that.
3. We **can't / may not** predict the kinds of jobs that this technology will create. No one knows what those jobs will be.
4. The health-care industry[1] is growing rapidly, so there **should / might not** be more jobs in that industry. That is one positive trend.
5. Jobs in retail stores **may / can't** be harder to find because more people will do their shopping online.
6. Actors **could / should** be replaced by robots in movies. It's possible.
7. Nurses **shouldn't / can't** have trouble finding jobs because there may be a shortage of nurses.
8. **Will / May** there be some jobs that will not exist in the future? Probably.
9. There **are not going to / may not** be mail carriers because everyone will probably use electronic documents.

[1]**industry:** the people and activities involved in a type of business

Classwork

2 Read the paragraph about a city. Then write sentences that make predictions about what life will be like in the city ten years from now. Use the words in parentheses and *could, should, shouldn't, might,* and *might not.* Sometimes more than one answer is possible.

The mayor of my city is making changes for the future. She wants to improve the quality of life for the residents. Recently the city began creating bike lanes for bicyclists and bus lanes for buses. The mayor hopes that there will be fewer cars on the streets, which should result in fewer car accidents and cleaner air. The city is also improving its parks. It is building a new community swimming pool, and it is creating more baseball and soccer fields. The city wants to build new, affordable housing because apartment rents are going up and the city's population is increasing. However, the mayor does not have the money to build more affordable housing now. She is trying to get new companies to move to the city, but real estate prices are high. She has not found a solution to the real estate problem yet.

Predictions: How Life in My City Will Change in 10 Years

1. *Air pollution should decrease.* (air pollution / decrease)
2. ______________________ (the number of bike riders / increase)
3. ______________________ (the number of traffic accidents / increase)
4. ______________________ (there / be / fewer cars on the streets)
5. ______________________ (rents / go up)
6. ______________________ (the population / increase)
7. ______________________ (new companies / move to the city)

Avoid Common Mistakes

1 Circle the mistakes.

1. Zack **can possibly call** (a) his mother tonight. He **could possibly call** (b) her tonight. He **may possibly send** (c) her an e-mail instead.
2. Family life **might be** (a) different in 10 years. Families **maybe** (b) bigger. Families **may be** (c) smaller.
3. **A:** How will health care change in the future? **B:** It **could get** (a) cheaper. Doctors **can be** (b) more helpful. Hospitals **might become** (c) more efficient.
4. Physical schools **may not exist** (a) in the future. Students **might not leave** (b) home to go to school. Teachers **couldn't interact** (c) with students. No one knows.
5. **A:** How will computers improve? **B:** They **could get** (a) faster. They **may get** (b) lighter. **A:** Will they get smaller? **B:** They **might get** (c).
6. **A:** I **might buy** (a) an electric car. **B:** My brother **may be** (b) buying one, too. Will they be cheaper in the future? **A:** Yes, they **may** (c).
7. **A:** Shawn **maybe** (a) in class right now. He **could be** (b) at work. Will he be home for dinner? **B:** He **might be** (c).
8. **A:** You **could possibly live** (a) to 100. I **must possibly live** (b) to 110. Do you want to retire early? **B:** I **might** (c).

2 Find and correct nine more mistakes in the article about transportation of the future.

Transportation of the **Future**

Cars ~~can~~ may not be part of our future. Instead, we maybe flying around in tiny private planes. In the future, gasoline must become hard to get. As a result, the kind of car we have today can become harder to use. Gasoline must become very expensive. Will other types of cars become common? Yes, they might become. Also, researchers think that small airplanes maybe common in the future. It's possible that these airplanes can run on power from the sun. They couldn't need any power at all. Who knows? If tiny personal planes become common, will houses have little home airports instead of garages? Yes, they might have.

Self-Assessment

HW

Circle the word or phrase that correctly completes each sentence.

1. The environment _____ in the future.

   a. different b. may be different c. must be different

2. Farms _____ more food in 20 years.

   a. can produce b. might produce c. must produce

3. I am sure that future communication _____ better than it was 10 years ago.

   a. should be b. is c. will be

4. Does he really think the population will be smaller 20 years from now? He _____ understand today's society.

   a. must not b. shouldn't c. mayn't

5. Changes in the environment _____ farming in the future. Experts are not sure.

   a. must affect b. affect c. might affect

6. The scientist's economic predictions _____ true. No one is sure.

   a. couldn't be b. might not be c. must not be

7. **A:** Are the results correct? **B:** They _____ . I haven't checked.

   a. might b. might correct c. might be

8. People _____ healthier food in the future. I'm sure of it.

   a. will eat b. eat c. might eat

9. Scientists are fairly certain that water _____ harder to get in the future.

   a. is b. must be c. should be

10. Cities of the future _____ good places to live.

    a. might not be b. mayn't be c. might be not

11. **A:** Are you going to dinner with us? **B:** Probably, but I _____ .

    a. will not b. should c. might not

12. **A:** Will cars use different fuel in the future? **B:** Yes, _____ .

    a. they should be b. they should c. they should use

13. A decline in the birthrate _____ be important in the future.

    a. could b. can c. must

14. The scientist _____ in the lab. He is usually there at this time of day.

    a. may not be b. should be c. are

15. Those statistics _____ correct. They look wrong to me.

    a. should be b. mightn't be c. can't be

1 b	7 c
2 b	8 a
3 c	9 c
4 a	10 a
5 c	11 c
6 b	12 b
	13 a
	14 b
	15 c

UNIT

24 Transitive and Intransitive Verbs; Verbs and Prepositions

Getting Along at Work

Transitive and Intransitive Verbs

1 Read the paragraph about loud co-workers. Are the verbs transitive or intransitive? Write *T* (transitive) or *I* (intransitive) above each verb in bold.

Loud co-workers **cause** (1) big problems. Studies by experts **show** (2) an interesting fact: One-third of workplace complaints are about loud co-workers. You and your co-workers can **feel** (3) better if you **follow** (4) some simple advice. First, try to **block** (5) the sound. **Use** (6) a music player with headphones or wear earplugs.[1] If you can't block the sound, **cover** (7) it. For example, the sound of a fan can **help** (8). The fan's noise **covers** (9) noise from your co-worker. Sometimes those things don't **solve** (10) the problem. Then you should **discuss** (11) the problem with the co-worker. Most people will **apologize** (12) and try to be quieter.

[1] **earplug:** a small object to put in your ears to protect them from sound

2 Read the paragraphs. Look at the verbs in bold. Underline each transitive verb. Circle each object.

When I **arrive** at the office each morning, I **walk** to the kitchen. I **make** a cup of coffee and say hello to my co-workers. After that, I **take** my coffee to my desk and **turn** on my computer. During the day, I **type** reports on my computer. I **play** music while I work. I always make sure to **keep** the volume low. That way if someone **knocks**, I can still **hear** them. I **eat** lunch with my co-workers. In the summer, we **eat** outside.

Everyone in my office gets along well. We don't **fight** or **argue**. It **helps** that there are only four of us! I **work** in a very small office. It's easy for us to **like** each other.

3 Complete the sentences about co-workers with the phrases in the box.

at her desk	loud music	the food
clearly	near a guy	~~things that distract me~~
headphones	something about the noise	to my office

1. Some of my co-workers do *things that distract me* .
2. I sit ________________ who likes to talk.
3. I can't think ________________ because of the noise.
4. Now, I come ________________ early to do work before he arrives.
5. One co-worker constantly plays ________________ .
6. She uses ________________ , but I can still hear the music.
7. Should I say ________________ to my boss?
8. Another co-worker eats ________________ instead of in the lunchroom.
9. I can smell ________________ and it distracts me.

4 Complete the sentences with information that is true for you. Use the transitive or intransitive form of verbs as indicated.

1. I will study *hard* . (Intransitive)
2. I will study *mathematics* . (Transitive)
3. I moved ________________ . (Intransitive)
4. I moved ________________ . (Transitive)
5. I can drive ________________ . (Intransitive)
6. I can drive ________________ . (Transitive)
7. I left ________________ . (Intransitive)
8. I left ________________ . (Transitive)

Verb + Object + Preposition Combinations

1 Complete the paragraph about workplace problems. Use *about, for, from, to,* or *with* and the correct form of the verbs in parentheses.

I am a waiter at a hotel. Politeness and appropriate behavior are two very important qualities for employees. Every new employee must attend training sessions. At these sessions, the manager *discusses* (1) (discuss) problems on the job *with* (1) everyone. You can _______ (2) (learn) a lot _______ (2) these meetings. The manager usually _______ (3) (explain) difficult situations _______ (3) us. Next, employees work in groups and decide on ways to handle the situations. Finally, we share ideas and explain how we would handle the problems with all kinds of people from all kinds of cultures. We _______ (4) (get) a lot of ideas _______ (4) the discussions. For example, when a guest is angry, we learn to stay calm and avoid becoming angry ourselves. If the customer is very upset, we _______ (5) (ask) the manager _______ (5) help. During work, we _______ (6) (remind) each other _______ (6) the things we learned at those meetings, and we often _______ (7) (ask) each other _______ (7) advice.

2 Unscramble the sentences about Gustavo, a new employee.

1. from his co-workers / Gustavo / learn / many things

   Gustavo learns many things from his co-workers.

2. help / him / with difficult tasks / his co-workers

   ____

3. ask / he / them / for advice

   ____

4. he / get / from them / good feedback

   ____

5. company policies / explain / they / to him

   ____

6. he / discuss / with them / problems

   ____

3 Write one or two sentences for each situation. Use verb + object + preposition combinations.

1. borrow something from someone

   I borrowed a pen from another student in my class.

2. explain something to someone

   ____

   ____

3. help someone with something

   ____

   ____

4. spend time with someone

   ____

   ____

5. ask someone for something

   ____

   ____

6. remind someone about something

   ____

   ____

8. learn something from someone

   ____

   ____

9. thank someone for something

   ____

   ____

Verb + Preposition Combinations

1 Complete the sentences about flex time. Circle the correct preposition that goes with each verb in bold.

Companies **count on / about** (1) their employees to work hard. Today's employees are often busy with many responsibilities in their personal lives. Some companies have **thought about / on** (2) ways to help these employees so that the employees can **deal about / with** (3) their responsibilities at home and on the job better. These companies have **talked to / at** (4) their employees and **listened about / to** (5) their concerns. Some employees have young children who **depend to / on** (6) them. Others have elderly parents who **count about / on** (7) them for help. These employees often need to **ask for / at** (8) time off to take care of their families. This creates a lot of stress. Some companies have started flex time for their employees. *Flex* means "flexible." With flex time, employees choose their hours. They do not have to **worry about / for** (9) being late or leaving early. For example, Heather is an employee who lives with her grandfather. He **relies for / on** (10) her to take care of him. Since the company started flex time, Heather does not have to **apologize at / for** (11) taking the time to take care of her family.

2 Complete the conversation with the correct prepositions.

Marie: Hi, Hussein. I was looking ______ (1) you. I wanted to apologize ______ (2) yelling at you.

Hussein: Don't worry ______ (3) it. Are you OK?

Marie: No, I'm not. I'm having a bad day. I asked ______ (4) a raise, and the manager almost laughed ______ (5) me. She depends ______ (6) me a lot, so I think I deserve a raise.

Hussein: Maybe she's having a bad day, too. She was arguing ______ (7) someone on the phone earlier. I've never seen her so angry.

Marie: Maybe I'll talk __to__ (8) her later about it. How's your day going?

Hussein: Well, I've been looking __for__ (9) a new job.

Marie: No way! You can't leave.

Hussein: I've thought __about__ (10) it for a while. Last week, I applied for a job, and I think I got it. Please don't tell anyone, OK?

Marie: You can count __on__ (11) me, but I hate to see you go.

Hussein: Thanks.

3 Answer the questions. Write sentences that are true for you. Classwork (?)

1. When you talk to a friend, what do you like to talk about?

   I like to talk about classes.

2. What kinds of movies do you usually laugh at?

   ____

3. Who do you rely on for help and support?

   ____

4. What do you often think about?

   ____

5. What do you often worry about?

   ____

6. Write one interesting thing that happened to you last year.

   ____

Avoid Common Mistakes

Classwork (?)

1 Circle the mistakes.

1. Peggy likes music, but she doesn't like to **hear it** (a) at work. Her office is in the same building as Pedro's, but she doesn't **know him** (b). Peggy has a small business. She **runs herself** (c).
2. All day, I **listen to** (a) Bill's phone calls. I **listen** (b) his conversations. I **listen to** (c) many calls.

3. I **discussed my work with** (a) my boss. We **discussed about** (b) a problem with a co-worker. I **explained the problem to** (c) her.
4. At work on Friday, Tom **wore on** (a) jeans. Pablo **wore** (b) a baseball cap. Marie **was wearing** (c) running shoes.
5. My co-worker and I **don't like each other** (a). I **don't like** (b). He **doesn't like me** (c).
6. I **asked** (a) company policies. I **asked about** (b) vacation policies. I **asked my boss for** (c) advice.
7. What am I **looking for** (a)? I'm **looking for** (b) more money. I'm **looking with** (c) a new job.
8. Haoran **drives** (a) a fast car. I **drive with** (b) a delivery truck. Luis **drives** (c) a motorcycle.

2 Find and correct eight more mistakes in the advertisement for PrivaPhones.

Do noises distract? Is it hard for you to deal on noisy co-workers? What can solve the problem? A set of PrivaPhones can solve! Just wear on PrivaPhones at work. You'll ask yourself, "What happened the noise?" With PrivaPhones, you won't hear. This lets you work with hard at your job. PrivaPhones depend new technology to protect your ears. Your PrivaPhones are waiting with you today!

Self-Assessment

Circle the word or phrase that correctly completes each sentence.

1. The worker next to me ____ bad-smelling perfume.

   a. wears to   b. wears   c. wears with

2. Hey, Lucas. Your package just ____.

   a. arrived   b. arrived it   c. arrived for

3. How many salespeople __c__ ?

   a. work b. work your office c. work at your office

* 4. The first president of our company __(a)__ for 20 years.

   a. ran it b. ran c. ran in

5. Is that your bag on this chair? Could you please __b__ ?

   a. move b. move it c. move in

6. My co-worker __c__ the office party.

   a. reminded about me b. reminded about c. reminded me about

7. I don't know what to do. Can I __a__ some advice?

   a. ask you for b. ask for you c. ask

8. That box looks really heavy. Let me __c__ it.

   a. help you b. help with you c. help you with

9. That's a difficult problem. Who are you going to __b__ ?

   a. discuss with it b. discuss it with c. discuss with

10. **A:** Do you plan to go to the company picnic? **B:** No. I __c__ , but I decided not to.

   a. thought for it b. thought it about c. thought about it

11. I haven't seen Mr. Brand lately. What __a__ him?

   a. happened to b. happened c. happened on

12. What did you and your co-workers __b__ ?

   a. talk b. talk about c. talk to

13. I need a new lamp for my desk. This one doesn't __c__ .

   a. work for b. work with c. work

14. Excuse me. Who does this office __c__ ?

   a. belong with b. belong c. belong to

15. I got a new desk for my office, but I __a__ .

   a. don't like it b. don't like c. don't

UNIT

25 Phrasal Verbs

Money, Money, Money

Intransitive Phrasal Verbs

1 Complete the sentences about the website. Circle the correct phrasal verbs.

Hungry Bob's Restaurant Reviews

home | help

Top Ten Sports Grill ★★★☆
American food and pizza.
Hamburgers are huge. TVs with sports events are everywhere.

1. I had an idea to make extra money, but it didn't **work out** / **work in**.
2. A lot of people **eat in** / **eat out** at restaurants. I started a website about the best restaurants.
3. I **went ahead** / **went in** and built the website.
4. It was great. I told people to **look out** / **look away** for bad restaurants.
5. The site gave information about things to **watch in** / **watch out** for, such as bad food and high prices.
6. I tried to sell advertising so the website could **go on** / **go out**.
7. Unfortunately, the economy was bad. Fewer people **went out** / **went in** to restaurants because of their finances.
8. Restaurants couldn't afford ads. My money **ran away** / **ran out**.
9. I couldn't **hang out** / **hang on** without money from ads.
10. I had to **give up** / **give away** and close the website.

2 Complete the sentences about buying a house. Use the particles in the box to make phrasal verbs that have the meaning in parentheses.

away	down	in	on	up
back	in	on	out	up

1. Many Americans want to buy a house after they grow _____ (become an adult).
2. When you buy a house, you have to watch __________ (be careful) for problems.
3. You may want to purchase a house right away, but hold __________ (wait).
4. Look carefully. Is the house in good condition? Does anything in the house look ready to break __________ (stop working)?
5. When you see a house with a big problem, turn around and go __________ (leave). You don't want a house like that.
6. Some buyers think the house price will go __________ (increase), so they want to buy right away.
7. This is bad. Don't let a fear of higher prices set __________ (begin and continue).
8. There is always another house. Hang __________ (wait).
9. When you find the perfect house, wait for a few days and then come __________ (return).
10. Do you still like it? Buy it at the best possible price, and then move __________ (begin living there).

3 Complete the paragraphs. Use the phrasal verbs in the boxes.

~~sit down~~	stand up	watch out	work out

A Some Americans don't get enough exercise. They sit all day at work, and then they come home and *sit down* (1) to watch TV. People who sit too much had better __________ (2) for health problems. Several times during the day, they should __________ (3) and walk around. Even better, they could join a health club and __________ (4) two or three times each week.

HW

give up　　got along　　grown up　　went on

B When I was a child, I got along (5) really well with Sam Brown, one of my neighbors. Sam's family did not have much money, but I didn't care. Our friendship went on (6) through elementary school and into high school. Now we have grown up (7) and gotten jobs, and we are still friends. Even if one of us makes a lot more money than the other, I know we will never give up (8) our friendship.

come back　　hangs on　　run out　　sets in

C Sometimes, money trouble sets in (9) and hangs on (10) for a long time. People run out (11) of money, and businesses can't sell things easily. Then, after a few years, good times come back (12), and the economy gets strong again.

Transitive Phrasal Verbs

1 A Unscramble the sentences. Then label the sentences *T* (transitive) or *I* (intransitive) according to the phrasal verbs in the sentences.

1. It makes sense to save money. (You / put / have to / some money / away / for the future)

   You have to put some money away for the future. ___*T*___

2. Save a little money each month. (It / add / will / up)

   ______________________________ ____

3. (Everyone / up / a bank account / should / set)

   ______________________________ ____

4. Banks pay you when you have an account with them. (That / your savings / up / helps to / build)

   ______________________________ ____

5. (You can / out / of the account at any time / take / your money)

   ______________________________ ____

B Label the phrasal verbs in bold *T* (transitive) or *I* (intransitive) according to their use in the sentences.

1. Most people have to **set up** a credit card account. You can't buy things online without one. _T_
2. However, you have to **work out** a way to **pay off** your credit card bills every month. _____ / _____
3. Don't **put off** your payments. If you're late, the card company will charge you an extra fee. _____
4. Stay with your payment plan and don't **give up**. _____

2 Complete the article about bank security. Choose the correct phrasal verbs. Change the verb form when necessary.

Is Your Money Safe?

A smart saver _puts away_ (1) (put away / write down) extra money in a bank to keep it safe. How do banks make sure that your money is safe? They have ________ (2) (bring up / figure out) several systems to do so. First, a bank hires security guards and ________ (3) (take out / work out) ways to catch robbers before they leave the bank. The bank ________ (4) (set up / pay back) a system of cameras, alarms, and human observers to see and catch bank robbers. Second, a bank has ways to ________ (5) (turn down / find out) the identity of anyone who tries to get money from an account. If you go to the bank to ________ (6) (take money out / bring money up) from your account, the bank will ask for an identity card with your picture on it. If you try to take money out online or at an ATM, the bank will ask for a secret passcode to ________ (7) (give up / find out) if you are really you. The bank also has other ways to keep your money safe. When you ________ (8) (add them up / give them up), you have a system that customers can trust.

3 Complete the conversations about money. Unscramble the words in A's questions. Then complete B's answers with an object pronoun and the phrasal verbs in parentheses. Sometimes more than one answer is possible.

1. **A:** My bank will give me a loan for college. Should I *take out this loan* OR *take this loan out* (this loan / take / out)?

   B: Sure. *Take it out* (take out).

2. **A:** Did you ______________________ (your student loans / pay / off)?

   B: No. I ______________________ (not / pay off).

3. **A:** I hear you plan to buy a car. Did you ______________________ (the costs / work / out) yet?

   B: Yes. I ______________________ (work out). It will cost a lot of money.

4. **A:** Do you sometimes ______________________ (paying a bill / put / off)?

   B: Actually, no. I prioritize bill payment. I ______________________ (not put off).

5. **A:** Could you please ______________________ (that music / turn / down)? I'm trying to work on my budget.

   B: Oh. Sorry. Sure, I can ______________________ (turn down).

4 Answer the questions about your budget. Write sentences that are true for you.

1. What is a good way to build up a savings account?

   A good way to build up a savings account is to save a little money every month.

2. When you want to find out some information about money, what do you do?

   ____

3. Have you worked out a budget? Why or why not?

   ____

4. When you want to save money, what do you give up?

   ____

5. Do you put away a little money every month? Why or why not?

   ____

6. Why did you take out a loan? If you haven't, will you take out a loan in the future?

   ____

Avoid Common Mistakes

1 Circle the mistakes.

1. I wanted to **set up a gym membership** (a), but I didn't have my ID with me. I couldn't **set up it** (b), so I had to **put off my workout** (c).
2. I have to **find** (a) a new bank. I have to **find out** (b) one near my apartment. I have to **find out** (c) if it is a good bank.
3. The pay from my job **fell down** (a) last year. I didn't **put away** (b) any money, so now I have to **work out** (c) a budget.
4. When the phone rang, I **picked it up** (a). It was my mother. But then the doorbell rang, so I had to **hang up the phone** (b). I had to **call back her** (c).
5. My mom's car **broke down** (a) again yesterday. It had only been two weeks since the last time her car **broke** (b). My mom **broke down** (c) in tears.
6. Don't **pick bad spending habits** (a). Don't **put bill payments off** (b) until tomorrow. Otherwise, your debt will **grow** (c).
7. Will the price of houses **rise** (a) in the future? Will the price of gas **go up** (b)? Will the price of food **rise up** (c)?
8. After you start a savings account, it will **grow up** (a). The money will **add up** (b). It will pay for college when your children **grow up** (c).

2 Find and correct seven more mistakes in the web article about paying for college.

Education Advice

Planning to Pay for College

Smart parents save money from their income for their children's college education. A smart parent puts ~~away it~~ it away in a college savings plan. This is a priority. A college savings plan will only work if you start early. You have to find ~~out~~ a good savings plan. You have to set up it before your child grows. You cannot build up it if you start too late. To decide how much money you need, find out how much a year of college costs now. Experts point out that the price of a college education rises ~~up~~ by about 8 percent every year. Do the math. The cost will grow ~~up~~ over the years.

Self-Assessment

Circle the word or phrase that correctly completes each sentence.

1. I will write __b__ .

   a. my down expenses (b.) my expenses down c. my expenses

2. When I __a__ , I didn't have a lot of money.

   (a.) came back from vacation b. came from vacation back c. came from back vacation

3. __c__ . I have to stop at the bank before we go to the restaurant.

   a. Give up b. Get along (c.) Hang on

4. Our car has __c__ . We need to buy a new one.

   a. broken b. broken in (c.) broken down

5. I wasn't sure about the cost, but then I __a__ .

   (a.) figured it out b. figured out it c. figured out

6. She saves everything. She never __b__ .

   a. throws away (b.) throws anything away c. anything throws away

7. Brian is ______ a customer service company in Chicago.

   a. setting up b. up setting c. setting with

8. I made a budget, but my plans didn't ______ .

   a. work it out b. work out c. out

9. **A:** You took out a loan for college, right? **B:** Yes, I did, but I ______ .

   a. paid it back b. paid c. paid back it

10. What kind of budget ______ ?

    a. did you set it up b. you did set up c. did you set up

11. **A:** Write down all your expenses. **B:** Why should I ______ ?

    a. write down b. write down them c. write them down

12. **A:** I go to restaurants at least twice a week. **B:** Really? I can't afford to ______ that often on my income.

    a. eat b. eat out c. eat it out

13. **A:** How's your restaurant doing? **B:** Great! It has really ______ .

    a. taken off b. taken c. taken it off

14. I didn't hear today's lecture on credit card debt. Can you please ______ for me?

    a. sum up it b. sum it c. sum it up

15. Unfortunately, Kelly has bad spending habits. I think she ______ in college.

    a. picked them up b. picked them c. picked up them

UNIT 26

Comparatives

We Are All Different

Comparative Adjectives and Adverbs

1 Complete the paragraph about siblings. Use the comparative form of the words in parentheses.

In some cultures, a first-born child has more rights than *younger* (young) siblings.
(1)
In earlier times, the law in many European countries treated first-born children better (good). When their parents died, the older (old)
(2) (3)
children were more likely (likely) to inherit[1] their parents' houses and
(4)
money. Without this property, younger (young) siblings had to work
(5)
harder (hard) to make a living. However, many young siblings did well.
(6)
They had weaker (weak) connections to a piece of land, so many of them
(7)
were were adventurous (adventurous). They were freer (free) to travel
(8) (9)
and learn new ideas. Many had better (good) educations than the average
(10)
person. This gave them stronger (strong) skills in business and other fields.
(11)
Some became more important (important) in the community than their siblings.
(12)

[1]**inherit:** get money, land, or other property from your parents after they die

2 A Read the interview about identical twins. Complete the sentences with the comparative form of the words in parentheses. Note that ↑ means *more* and ↓ means *less*.

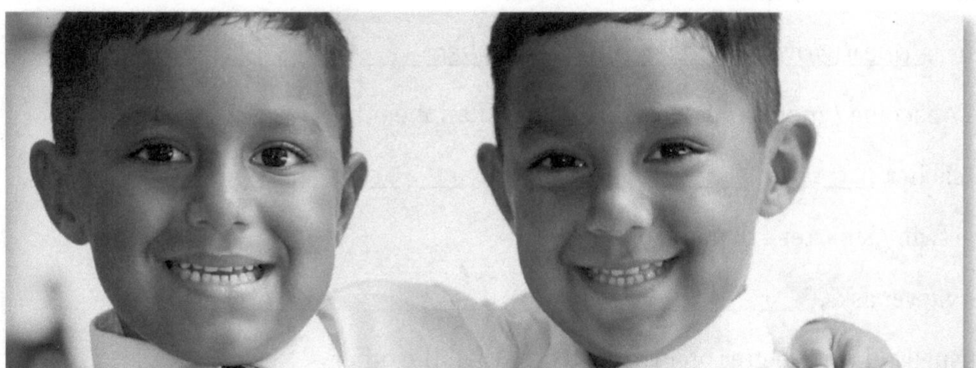

HW

Kyle: Our guest today is Dr. Marta Torres, director of the psychology department at Tilldale College. Dr. Torres is an expert on twin psychology. Hi, Dr. Torres.

Marta: Hello. Nice to be here.

Kyle: Dr. Torres, if identical twins have the same genes, why are some of them so different?

Marta: Do you mean their personalities? Often, one twin is *friendlier* (1) (↑ friendly), or maybe one is less easygoing (2) (↓ easygoing).

Kyle: Right, but is there a reason for that?

Marta: Researchers think that it's mostly because they have different experiences. One twin might be more confident (3) (↑ confident) than the other because her teachers were nicer (4) (↑ nice). The greater confidence might make her more independent (5) (↑ independent) and help her succeed. The other twin might have different experiences that make her less successful (6) (↓ successful).

Kyle: Can one twin be smarter (7) (↑ smart) than the other?

Marta: I don't know. What does "smarter" mean? People who study the psychology of twins have different views about that. One twin can be more educated (8) (↑ educated), and she might seem more intelligent (9) (↑ intelligent). Does she really have a better (10) (↑ good) brain? I don't think so, unless the other twin had an accident, or a worse (11) (↑ bad) diet, or something like that.

Kyle: That's all the time we have. Thank you, Dr. Torres. I understand twins a lot better (12) (↑ good) now.

Marta: My pleasure.

B Unscramble the sentences. Use the information from the interview in A to help you.

1. is friendlier / one twin / than the other

   Sometimes, *one twin is friendlier than the other*.

2. can help / become / more confident / one twin / than the other

   A nicer teacher ______________________.

3. can / one twin / smarter / than the other / be

   The interviewer asks, "______________________?"

4. doesn't usually / have a better brain / one twin / than the other

   According to Dr. Torres, ______________________.

5. can affect / a better diet / the brain

   According to Dr. Torres, ______________________.

Comparatives with *As . . . As*

1 Complete the sentences with *as . . . as* and the words in parentheses.

1. When I was younger, I was an average student. Most students did better than I did.

   My grades were not *as good as* (good) most students' grades.

2. Also, I was less athletic than other students.

   I was not as athletic as (athletic) other students.

3. In tenth grade, I played basketball, but not very well. The other players were better.

   I was not as fast as (fast) the other players on my team.

4. I could play the piano a little, but I wasn't in the school band.

   I was not as skilled as (skilled) the students who played in concerts.

5. Now that I'm older, I feel better about my abilities.

   At the magazine where I work, most of the other writers are not as experienced as (experienced) I am.

6. They don't write as well as (well) I do.

7. I am not the best writer in the world, but I'm as creative as (creative) the writers for big national magazines. I've come a long way!

2 A Look at the student biographies. Complete the sentences with (*not*) *as . . . as* and the words in parentheses.

Name: *Naresh*
Age: *21*
Gender: *male*
Height: *6 feet, 2 inches*
Weight: *185 pounds*
Hair color: *black*
Size of hometown: *about 35,000 people*
Education: *finishing degree from Crimson Junior College (9,000 students)*
Grade point average: *3.68*
Sports: *played basketball for his college*

Name: *Mariana*
Age: *18*
Gender: *female*
Height: *5 feet, 6 inches*
Weight: *120 pounds*
Hair color: *black*
Size of hometown: *about 35,000 people*
Education: *ending first year at Tilldale College (1,700 students)*
Grade point average: *3.68*
Sports: *plays tennis for her college*

1. Mariana is *not as old as* (old) Naresh.
2. Naresh is not as short as (short) Mariana.
3. Mariana does not weigh as much as (much) Naresh.
4. Naresh's hair is as dark as (dark) Mariana's hair.
5. Mariana's hometown is as big as (big) Naresh's hometown.
6. Naresh's college is not as small as (small) Mariana's college.
7. Naresh's grade point average is as high as (high) Mariana's grade point average.
8. Mariana is as interested in sports as (interested in sports) Naresh.

B Write more (*not*) *as . . . as* sentences about Naresh and Mariana. Write at least three negative sentences.

1. *Naresh is not as young as Mariana.*
2. ______
3. ______
4. ______
5. ______
6. ______
7. ______

HW

3 Write sentences using (*not*) *as . . . as* that are true for people you know. Use the words in parentheses.

1. (skilled) *I am not as skilled as my brother at playing the piano.*
2. (talented) ______
3. (young) ______
4. (old) ______
5. (intelligent) ______
6. (strong) ______
7. (kind) ______

Avoid Common Mistakes

HW

1 Circle the mistakes.

1. I have one sister. She's a **good sister** (a). She's a **better sister** (b). She's a **helpful sister** (c).
2. My brother's **younger that** (a) me. He's **taller than** (b) me. He's not **smarter than** (c) me.
3. Tom's family is **larger than** (a) my family. My family is **more smaller than** (b) his family. Thuy's family is **bigger than** (c) both families.
4. Kim is **as interested** (a) in the class **as** (a) Ben is. He likes it **as much as** (b) she does. I'm not **as interested** (c) they are.
5. Our Spanish teacher is **friendly** (a). She is **less serious** (b). Her personality is **nice** (c).

1 b
2 a
3 b
4 c
5 b
6 c
7 b
8 a

6. Thuy's family is **richer than** (a) Jack's family. Thuy went to **more expensive schools than** (b) Jack did. Thuy's house is **bigger that** (c) Jack's house.

7. You always seem **busier than** (a) I am. Your work is **more better than** (b) my work. You are **more hardworking than** (c) I am.

8. Is Pete **as talented** (a) his twin sister? Is he **as smart as** (b) her? Do you think he'll be **as successful as** (c) she is?

2 Find and correct eight more mistakes in the website article about the new semester.

Academic Programs | Future Students | Current Students

Jacob County Community College

The New Semester Is Starting!

The president's office announces a newer admissions policy for the families of current students at Jacob County Community College. It will now be more easier for siblings of current students to apply. The application form for these siblings is much shorter that the normal application. Also, siblings of current students can apply earlier that usual. The college's president, Wayne Roberts, said, "We want to be as open possible to the families of our students." He explained that "legacy admissions" – special procedures for students' relatives – are becoming more commoner at colleges. Roberts explained that the college's approval of sibling applications does not take as long usual. "Siblings are alike in many ways," he said. "If a student is already doing well here, brothers or sisters will probably succeed, too." The college hopes the newer policy will make admissions simpler and more quicker.

Self-Assessment

Circle the word or phrase that correctly completes each sentence.

1. First-born children are _____ than their siblings.

   a. confident b. more confident c. as confident

2. My friend Gary can sing _____ than most people.

   a. betterly b. more well c. better

3. We need to hire someone who is _____ Erin.

   a. more responsible that b. responsibler than c. more responsible than

4. Twins choose the same careers _____ than other siblings.

   a. more often b. more oftener c. more oftenly

5. My twin brother moved to Florida from New York. He likes _____ weather.

   a. more hot b. hotter c. hoter

6. Erin makes friends more easily than Gary because she is _____ .

   a. funnier b. funnyer c. more funnier

7. My father was _____ than my Uncle Don.

   a. independenter b. independent c. more independent

8. I think that most people my parents' age are _____ most people my age.

   a. less tall as b. not as tall as c. less shorter than

9. My youngest sibling works _____ in school as I do.

   a. as hard b. harder than c. hard

10. Teenagers are usually _____ adults.

    a. as more careful as b. not as careful than c. not as careful as

11. My professor said that younger siblings are usually _____ first-borns.

    a. more independent than b. as independenter than c. independenter than

12. Is Bruce _____ Erin?

    a. taller b. taller than c. tall than

13. Tom _____ most other students.

    a. talks than b. talks more louder than c. talks louder than

14. You write _____ than anyone else I know.

(a.) more beautifully   b. beautifuller than   c. as beautifully

15. I want to have Mr. Barton as my teacher. He's _____ Ms. Farmer.

a. less seriously than   (b.) less serious than   c. less serious as

1b
2c
3c
4a
5b
6a
7c

8b
9a
10c
11a
12b
13c
14a
15b

UNIT

27 Superlative Adjectives and Adverbs

The Best and the Worst

Superlative Adjectives and Adverbs

1 Read the paragraphs about hurricanes. Complete the sentences with the superlative form of the words in parentheses.

Deadly Hurricanes

Hurricane Katrina was the most costly (1) (costly) storm in U.S. history. It did more than $80 billion in damage. In one way, however, Katrina was not __________ (2) (bad) hurricane to hit the United States. __________ (3) (dangerous) hurricane was "The Great Galveston Hurricane" that struck Texas in 1900. About 8,000 people died.

Strong Winds

__________ (4) (high) wind speed recorded in a hurricane was around 200 miles per hour (mph). That was during Hurricane Camille in 1969. Actually, __________ (5) (honest) thing to say about Camille is that scientists aren't sure about its wind speeds because the technology failed. At 200 mph, the storm broke the recording equipment. __________ (6) (strong) winds were probably higher than that. However, __________ (7) (intense) wind ever measured in the United States was not in a hurricane at all. It was a wind of 231 mph on Mount Washington in the state of New Hampshire.

Hurricane Categories

Weather experts put hurricanes into groups called "categories."

________________ (8) (violent) storms, with winds over 155 mph, are in Category 5. ________________ (9) (weak) hurricanes are in Category 1, with winds between 74 and 95 mph. A wind speed of 74 mph is ________________ (10) (low) that a hurricane can have.

2 Complete the sentences about a student's research project. Use the superlative form with the words in parentheses. Note that ↑ means *most* and ↓ means *least.*

I'm doing a project on natural disasters. I wanted to find out which is the worst natural disaster (1) (↑ bad / natural disaster). Before I did any research, I thought hurricanes were ________________ (2) (↑ scary / ones) and floods were ________________ (3) (↓ interesting / ones).

Here are some of the facts I have discovered:

- Earthquakes ________________ (4) (occur / ↑ quickly) of all natural disasters. They only last a few seconds.
- Floods ________________ (5) (happen / ↑ frequently) of all natural disasters. Many people have experienced floods.
- Hurricanes are ________________ (6) (↑ predictable / natural disasters). Meteorologists ________ (7) hurricanes ________________ (7) (forecast / ↑ easy) of all natural disasters.

After I finished my report, I decided that people can ________ (8) hurricanes ________________ (8) (avoid / ↑ easily), but people can ________ (9) earthquakes ________________ (9) (avoid / ↓ easily). So now hurricanes are ________________ (10) (↓ scary / natural disaster) to me. Earthquakes are ________________ (11) (↑ terrifying / natural disaster).

I ________________ (12) (worked / ↑ hard) on this project of all the work I've done this semester. I am hoping to receive ________________ (13) (↑ good / grade). I think natural disasters are ________________ (14) (↑ interesting / subject) I've studied!

3 Read the information about tornadoes in the United States. Then answer the questions with superlatives.

U.S. Tornado Facts	
States where tornadoes happen often (1950–2004)	Texas (134 tornadoes), Oklahoma (58), Kansas (56)
States where tornadoes do not happen often (1950–2004)	Alaska (2), Rhode Island (9)
Month with most tornadoes (U.S. total)	May 2003 – 543 tornadoes
Months with most tornadoes (yearly average, 1955–1999)	May (180), June (171), April (109)
Day with the most tornadoes	April 4, 1974 – 147
Widest tornado	2.5 miles
Wind speed	probably about 300 miles per hour
Property damage from one tornado	perhaps $1 billion

1. Where do tornadoes happen most often?

   Tornadoes happen most often in Texas.

2. Where do tornadoes happen least often?

   ____

3. Which month and year had the largest number of tornadoes?

   ____

4. On average, in which month do tornadoes happen most often?

   ____

5. What was the largest number of tornadoes in one day?

____

6. What was the width of the widest tornado?

____

7. What was the fastest wind speed in a tornado?

____

8. What was the highest amount of property damage from one tornado?

____

Avoid Common Mistakes

1 Circle the mistakes.

1. Of all the cities in our area, Newtown **has the best storm shelters**.[1] (a) Its emergency services are **the efficientest** (b). They spend **the most generously** (c) on safety systems.
2. After the storm, the Grand City relief workers helped **the least quickly** (a). They did **the worst** (b). Templeton's workers did **the wellest** (c).
3. Felipe brought **him best** (a) workers to help at the site. They brought **their newest** (b) equipment. Building new shelters was **their most important** (c) role.
4. John explained **the storm the best** (a). He analyzed **the most clearly the storm** (b). We can understand **his report the most easily** (c).
5. High winds were **the frighteningest** (a) part of the storm. People outside were in **the greatest** (b) danger. Strong buildings were **the safest** (c) places to be.
6. Malaria is **the worst** (a) disease in that area. Mosquitoes are the **most dangerous** (b) health problem. Also, the people there have **the baddest** (c) medical care in the country.
7. Some relief workers did not do **their best** (a) work. They did not give **their most complete** (b) attention to the job. I can see, however, that you did **you best** (c) work.
8. The **greatest** (a) number of earthquakes in the United States happen in Alaska. The **strongest** (b) earthquake happened in Alaska in 1964. The **destructivest** (c) earthquake happened in California in 1906.

[1] **storm shelter:** a place to go for safety during a storm

2 Find and correct the mistakes in the web article about snowstorms.

Snowstorms

When we talk about the topic of weather, we should not forget snowstorms. One of the baddest snowstorms in history hit the United States and Canada in March 1993. At it strongest point, the storm reached from Canada to Central America. The eastern United States was hit the baddest. The storm affected the most seriously that area. The surprisingest snowfall was in Florida, which got about four inches. The storm dumped it heaviest snow – 69 inches – on the town of Mount LeConte, Tennessee. Tornadoes were one of the dangerousest aspects of the storm. They hit the hardest Florida. Because it was the violentest storm in more than 100 years, many people in the eastern United States call it "The Storm of the Century."

Self-Assessment

Circle the word or phrase that correctly completes each sentence.

1. Cell phones are ______ way to call for help in a major disaster.

   a. fastest b. the fastest c. the fast

2. The storm brought ______ snow of the season.

   a. the heaviest b. the heavy c. heaviest

3. This summer was the ______ one we've ever had.

   a. hotest b. most hot c. hottest

4. Sometimes, airplanes are ______ way for relief workers to reach places where disasters happen.

   a. the easyest b. the easiest c. an easiest

5. The police from this town reached the fire ______.

   a. the quickliest b. the most quickly c. the quick

6. All of the doctors are good, but Dr. Martin is _c_.

   a. the goodest b. the bestest (c.) the best

HW

7. I work _a_ when I am under a lot of pressure.

   (a.) best b. wellest c. goodest

8. Ken is _b_ the best relief workers on our team.

   a. one (b.) one of c. some of

9. Internet ads and social networking sites are _c_ ways to raise money.

   a. the effectivest b. the most (c.) the most effective

10. New Orleans was hit _a_ by that hurricane.

    (a.) the worst b. the bad c. the baddest

11. The relief workers did _c_ in the most dangerous situations.

    a. they best b. them best (c.) their best

12. The workers repaired the buildings the quickest. The workers fixed _a_.

    (a.) them the most rapidly b. them the rapidly c. the most rapidly them

13. After a storm, boats are sometimes _c_ way to carry relief supplies.

    a. the fastliest b. fast (c.) the fastest

14. That was _b_ tornado in history.

    a. the damaging (b.) the most damaging c. the damagingest

15. Relief workers are _____ hardest-working people I know.

    a. one of the (b.) some of the c. some of

6. c
7. a
8. b
9. c
10. a
11. c
12. a
13. c
14. b
15. b

UNIT

28

Gerunds and Infinitives (1)

Managing Time

Verbs Followed by Gerunds or Infinitives

1 Complete the paragraph about months with the gerund or infinitive form of the verbs in parentheses.

Early attempts to keep time involved _using_ (1) (use) natural events that occur regularly. Early humans noticed that the size of the moon seemed ________________ (2) (increase) and decrease every month. The time period from one full moon to the next is a month. Every society needed ________________ (3) (measure) that time period. Some societies decided ________________ (4) (use) the exact length of the moon's full cycle, which is 29 days, 12 hours, 44 minutes, and 3 seconds. However, other societies avoided ________________ (5) (use) this exact time period. They wanted ________________ (6) (calculate) time in a less specific way and in a way that followed the seasons. These societies decided ________________ (7) (measure) a month in whole days. Months like this tend ________________ (8) (be) 28 to 31 days long. In Western cultures, for example, people agreed ________________ (9) (follow) a calendar with seven months of 31 days, four months of 30 days (April, June, September, and November), and one month (February) of 28 or 29 days.

2 Unscramble the sentences about volunteer work. Use the gerund or infinitive form of the verbs in bold.

send | attach | save draft | forward | close

Date: 10-18-2011

To: Nick Soares

From: Jen Berg

Subject: Volunteering your time

Hi Nick,

1. **give** / would you ever consider / some of your time to do volunteer work

   Would you ever consider giving some of your time to do volunteer work?

2. as a volunteer at a kitchen for homeless people / **start** / I plan

   ____

3. it will involve / about four hours a week with a team at the shelter / **spend**

   ____

4. this because homeless people are really just like you and me / **do** / I decided

   ____

5. many people need help while they keep / for work / **look**

   ____

6. **spend** / they need / their time on job searches, not on searches for food

   ____

7. independent / **be** / they want

   ____

8. I can't refuse / a few hours every week / **give**

   ____

9. **donate** / if you want / some of your time, I can give you the shelter's number

   ____

10. these people / **help** / I think you will enjoy

    ____

— Jen

3 Read the conversation between Jeff and Meg. Complete the sentences with the gerund or infinitive form of the verbs in parentheses.

Jeff: Oh, no! It's after ten o'clock. I need *to run* (1) (run) to class, Meg. I'm going to be late!

Meg: Wait! It's not after ten. It's just after nine, Jeff. You keep ________ (2) (get) the time wrong.

Jeff: Oh. Yeah, I know. I seem ________ (3) (be) confused since my vacation in Michigan. The time is an hour later there. My body refuses ________ (4) (change) back to Chicago time.

Meg: You know, you can avoid ________ (5) (have) a problem. You can set your watch to the right time.

Jeff: I already have. I expected that ________ (6) (solve) the problem, but it didn't.

Meg: Maybe you should consider ________ (7) (see) a doctor.

Jeff: No, no, it's not that bad. I have to keep ________ (8) (try) to deal with it.

Meg: Well, I suggest ________ (9) (spend) more time outside.

Jeff: Why? I don't mind ________ (10) (be) outside, but . . .

Meg: It's the sunlight. People tend ________ (11) (deal) with time changes better if they are out in the sun.

Jeff: OK. I'll plan ________ (12) (study) outside later today. I'll be in front of the library.

Meg: Well, good. Maybe I'll join you. I hope ________ (13) (see) you there.

Verbs Followed by Gerunds and Infinitives

1 Complete the sentences with the verbs in parentheses. Use the gerund or infinitive form of the second verb. Make each sentence match the meaning of the previous statement in bold. Sometimes more than one answer is possible.

1. **Dan was doing something, and then he looked at the clock.**

   Dan *stopped to look* (stop / look) at the clock.

2. **Beth asked us to meet at noon. Later, she remembered that she asked us.**

   Beth ________________ (remember / ask) us to meet at noon.

3. **Felipe asked everyone to come to a meeting on Thursday, but everyone was busy.**

   Felipe ______________________ (try / plan) the meeting for Thursday, but he wasn't able to.

4. **I wanted to set my alarm clock, but I didn't do it.**

   I ______________________ (forget / set) my alarm clock.

5. **I spend an hour each day playing video games.**

   I ______________________ (love / play) video games.

6. **How was your trip to Japan? Did you change your watch to the correct time?**

   Did you ______________________ (remember / change) your watch?

7. **My neighbor makes noise until 1:00 or 2:00 in the morning.**

   I wish he would ______________________ (stop / make) noise.

8. **Heather can't fall asleep. She took a warm bath. She still couldn't fall asleep.**

   Heather ______________________ (try / take) a warm bath to fall asleep, but it didn't work.

2 Complete the sentences about Jordan's work history with the verbs in parentheses. Use the gerund or infinitive form of the second verb. Sometimes more than one answer is possible.

1. Jordan _*finished going*_ (finished / go) to Dana Community College last year.
2. In his student adviser job, he ______________________ (liked / help) students find solutions for time-management problems.
3. He ______________________ (started / work) on a bachelor's degree at a university.
4. He ______________________ (enjoys / work) for large companies.
5. He also ______________________ (started / volunteer) at a school two years ago.
6. He ______________________ (wanted / teach) more people about time management.
7. Now Jordan is working for a management company. He ______________________ (tries / train) employees to be more efficient in their jobs.
8. Jordan ______________________ (loves / work) at his new job because he creates the training materials.

Avoid Common Mistakes

1 Circle the mistakes.

1. Iman **hopes to be** (a) a nurse. She **enjoys to study** (b). She **wants to finish** (c) school quickly.
2. I **considered to change** (a) my class schedule. I **want to have** (b) later classes. I **need to sleep** (c) more.
3. Jim **enjoyed traveling** (a) to Europe. He **expected feel** (b) tired. He didn't **mind having** (c) jetlag.
4. Time **seems going** (a) faster as you get older. Children **tend to think** (b) that a year is long. To their parents, it **seems to pass** (c) quickly.
5. I **have finished planning** (a) my trip to Peru. I **plan to stay** (b) in Lima. I **hope be** (c) there for six months.
6. Matt **denies to be** (a) late for class. His teacher **refuses to believe** (b) him. Do you **recall seeing** (c) him?
7. I know I gave you a class schedule. I **remember giving** (a) it to you. I **recall to do** (b) that last Tuesday. I **did not forget to give** (c) it to you.
8. I **stopped reading** (a) that book. I know I should read more, and I **keep trying** (b). I **tried read** (c) more last night.

2 Find and correct eight more mistakes in the letter about Kate's new job.

Hi Sam,

I wanted ~~writing~~ *to write* to you last week, but I didn't have time. Sorry, but I got really busy and forgot writing. I enjoy to be in San Diego, but I don't have much time for fun. I expected working only eight hours yesterday, but I kept to work at the office for eleven hours. Every day, I finish to do one thing, and then I have to do another. Last Sunday, I had some free time, so I decided take a bus to a beach just north of San Diego. I expected see sand, but it was very rocky and really pretty. Well, I should stop to write now. If you get the time, come visit!

Love,

Kate

Self-Assessment

Circle the word or phrase that correctly completes each sentence.

1. I expected _____ more time to finish my work.

   a. having b. to have c. have

2. Why do you keep _____ at the clock?

   a. to look b. look c. looking

3. I suggested _____ more flexible about our employees' work schedule.

   a. being b. be c. to be

4. The school expects _____ on time for every class.

   a. you b. you to be c. you be

5. I agreed _____ my roommate before 8:00 a.m.

   a. not waking up b. to wake not up c. not to wake up

6. Sometimes I need to stop and _____ time with my children.

   a. spend b. spending c. to spend

7. I considered waiting and _____ a later flight.

   a. to take b. take c. taking

8. I remember _____ the appointment this morning.

   a. to make b. making c. make

9. I forgot _____ my alarm, so I woke up an hour late this morning.

   a. to set b. set c. setting

10. Josh's parents try _____ how long he watches TV.

    a. control b. to c. to control

11. Professor Brand's class seems _____ really long because it is so boring.

    a. being b. to be c. be

12. You should stop _____ video games. You have to spend some time on your homework.

    a. to play b. play c. playing

13. Children tend _____ that time goes slowly.

    a. to think b. think c. thinking

14. The coach expects _____ for an hour every day.

    a. us run b. us running c. us to run

15. I don't mind _____ late.

    a. to arrive b. arriving c. arrive

UNIT 29

Gerunds and Infinitives (2)

Civil Rights

More About Gerunds

1 Complete the paragraphs about older workers. Use the gerund form of the verbs in the boxes.

~~get~~	hire	lose	work

The civil rights movement of the 1960s succeeded in *getting* (1) the U.S. government to pass the Age Discrimination in Employment Act (ADEA) in 1967. The law states that not ___ (2) older people because of their age is illegal. Some older workers are worried about ___ (3) their jobs to younger workers. A recent survey showed that 70 percent of older people plan to keep on ___ (4) in their 70s.

be	do	give	read

Tracy is 50 years old and is a paralegal at a law firm. She is not afraid of ___ (5) too old for her job because she loves her job and is very good at ___ (6) it. She never gets tired of ___ (7) about new laws and court cases. She is also helpful to new, younger paralegals. Her boss recognizes how valuable she is. He is thinking of ___ (8) her a raise.

2 **A** Circle the correct preposition next to each adjective or verb and write it.

1. afraid *of* — about — in — (of)
2. aware ___ — about — for — of
3. forget ___ — about — in — on
4. important ___ — about — for — of
5. involved ___ — in — of — on
6. keep ___ — about — of — on
7. sorry ___ — about — in — on
8. think ___ — about — for — in
9. worried ___ — about — in — of

B Complete the conversation about a sales team. Use the words in parentheses with the prepositions you wrote in A. Write the gerund form of the verbs in bold.

Elena: Sales are *important for keeping* (1) (important / **keep**) our business strong.

Ted: I agree, but I'm ______ (2) (worried / not **have**) enough good salespeople.

Ashley: Excuse me. I've been ______ (3) (involved / **interview**) many young people. We have some nice young candidates with a lot of energy.

Elena: Only young candidates? Isn't that age discrimination?

Ashley: Well, we have to ______ (4) (think / **reach**) many companies all over the country. Traveling takes a lot of time and energy.

Jason: But we shouldn't ______ (5) (forget / **need**) experience in our sales force as well.

Elena: Yes, Jason, you're right. I also think we need to be ______ (6) (aware / **create**) the right image of our company. Older salespeople make customers feel that we are trustworthy and reliable.

Ashley: You're right, but we also have to ______ (7) (worry / **seem**) too old.

Ted: I'm 67. Am I too old? I'm ______ (8) (sorry / **disagree**) with you on this, but I do feel some discrimination here.

Ashley: OK. Sorry, Ted. Still, many companies think that young workers have more energy and experience with current technology.

Jason: So I guess you're ______ (9) (afraid / **not look**) modern or innovative.

Elena: Well, yes. Our customers need to feel sure that we have the latest products. However, we can't be ______ (10) (involve / **discriminate**) against anyone – not against older people and not against younger people. We just have to look for the best salespeople.

More About Infinitives

1 **A** Circle each infinitive after the verb *be.*

The main goal of the Americans with Disabilities Act (ADA) is to prevent discrimination against disabled persons. An important purpose of the law is to make sure that entrances include ramps and elevators so that disabled persons can enter the buildings. This law benefits the American economy in several ways. One way is to let disabled persons contribute their skills to companies. Another benefit is to allow disabled persons to support themselves.

B Circle each infinitive that shows purpose.

Researchers have conducted many studies to understand left-handedness better. A left-handed person uses the left hand, not the right, to do most everyday tasks. However, only about 11 percent of the world's people are left-handed. They face a kind of discrimination because most products are made to be convenient for right-handed people. Supporters of left-handers' rights have written to many manufacturers in order to get more scissors, keyboards, guitars, and other products for left-handers.

2 Read the paragraph about housing discrimination. Answer the questions with the infinitive form of the verbs in parentheses.

The year was 1952. Matt was a white man. He wanted to find a house for sale. Jeff, who was African American, had the same goal. They felt that it was important to live in a nice neighborhood. They both liked Linden. Matt and Jeff both called real estate agents. Matt's agent worked hard to find him houses. On the other hand, Jeff's agent acted differently. Her job was to help people find homes in Linden, but she believed that African Americans should not live there. She said no houses were for sale. She lied to keep him out of Linden. This story shows one thing that some people did to segregate African Americans from whites in the United States years ago. It took many years to change people's minds about discrimination.

1. What was Matt's and Jeff's goal? (find)

   Their goal was to find a house for sale __________.

2. What was important to them? (live)

   It was important ______________________________________.

3. Was Matt's agent helpful? (find)

   Yes, he worked hard ______________________________________.

4. What was Jeff's agent's job? (help)

   Her job was ______________________________________.

5. Why did Jeff's agent lie? (keep)

   She lied ______________________________________.

6. What took many years? (change)

   It took many years ______________________________________.

3 Complete the statements with infinitives. Write sentences that are true for you.

1. I would like to organize people to *help the homeless* ____________________.
2. In today's world, it seems difficult to ______________________________.
3. Some people are fighting in order to ______________________________.
4. Today, we need someone to work hard to ______________________________.

Avoid Common Mistakes

1 Circle the mistakes.

1. Discriminating against people **is** (a) wrong. Segregating them **are** (b) wrong, too. Treating them fairly **is** (c) right.
2. We are **interested for** (a) helping disabled people. We **believe in** (b) protecting their rights. We will **keep on fighting** (c) for them.
3. I'm **sorry about missing** (a) the meeting. Did you **talk about to demonstrate** (b) for civil rights? I should **be involved in planning** (c) the demonstration.
4. The purpose of the dinner is **to help** (a) with Pete's run for mayor. Our purpose is **to raise** (b) money from people at the dinner. The purpose of Pete's speech is **for to thank** (c) his supporters.
5. Sometimes, it's **hard treat** (a) people fairly. It's **difficult to think** (b) of other people's feelings. Still, it's **important to respect** (c) others.

6. Protecting farm workers **were** (a) difficult. Working long hours **was** (b) common for them. Getting paid poorly **was** (c) normal.
7. I **believe in** (a) helping people get good jobs. I **forget of** (b) seeing them as black or white, old or young. I **think about** (c) their abilities, not their appearance.
8. Ms. Parks was **aware of to live** (a) with an unfair system. She was **tired of standing** (b) to please other people. Her decision to stay in her bus seat was **important in helping** (c) African Americans.

2 Find and correct eight more mistakes in the announcement about a college's rights club.

The College Rights Club

Working for civil rights ~~are~~ *is* everyone's duty. The College Rights Club invites all students to be involved for ending discrimination. Please join us at our next meeting on October 7 in the Student Union. We will talk about to plan this year's activities. Last year, we worked hard for to protect the rights of people on campus. We believed was important to get better access to campus buildings for disabled persons. Supporting workers on local farms were also an important project. We succeeded about setting up a Farm Workers' Aid Center to provide day-care for workers' children. This year, we will keep on to help all members of our community to be treated fairly and respectfully. We hope you believe it is important for to be part of this effort. Join us!

Self-Assessment

Circle the word or phrase that correctly completes each sentence.

1. We can change society by _____ discrimination.

   a. end b. ending c. to end

2. Paying workers too little money _____ wrong.

   a. is b. are c. am

3. Americans should not forget about _____ to protect civil rights.

   a. fight b. to fight c. fighting

4. One necessary thing for some disabled workers _____ an accessible place to work.

   a. finding b. is finding c. to find

5. I believe in _____ a good day's work for a good day's pay.

   a. doing b. to do c. for doing

6. Many older Americans say their goal is _____ working in their 70s and 80s.

   a. keep b. kept c. to keep

7. In the past, some African Americans had to struggle in order _____ .

   a. voting b. to vote c. vote

8. In some places, it once cost money _____ . This was illegal, but it happened anyway.

   a. to vote b. voting c. in voting

9. _____ children of all racial groups become friends was part of Dr. King's dream.

   a. He sees b. See c. Seeing

10. César Chávez worked _____ equal rights for Mexican Americans.

    a. to get b. for get c. getting

11. Some employers say they are worried about _____ older, experienced workers.

    a. for to lose b. losing c. to lose

12. When you want to change people's minds, it is important _____ to them respectfully.

    a. speak b. speaking c. to speak

13. For older workers looking for jobs, the hardest thing is _____ against younger people.

    a. competing b. compete c. for compete

14. In 1963, at least 200,000 people marched to the White House _____ equal rights.

    a. support b. for supporting c. to support

15. It takes time _____ people's attitudes toward equal rights.

    a. changing b. to change c. change

UNIT 30 Subject Relative Clauses (Adjective Clauses with Subject Relative Pronouns)

Sleep

Subject Relative Clauses

1 Complete the article about children and sleep. Use *who/that* for people and *that/which* for things with the correct form of the verbs in parentheses. Sometimes more than one answer is possible.

Maybe you know a teenager <u>*who sleeps* OR *that sleeps*</u> (1) (sleep) very late in the morning. Researchers ______________ (2) (study) sleep say that this is normal. People ______________ (3) (be) from 13 to 19 years of age need 9 or 10 hours of sleep each night.

Scientists have identified different stages of a person's early life ______________ (4) (have) different sleep patterns. The first stage, when you're a baby, is the only stage ______________ (5) (not / have) a regular pattern. Babies sleep at different times from day to day, sometimes for as many as 18 hours. However, children ______________ (6) (be) between one and three years old (the toddler stage) usually sleep about 12 to 15 hours a day. Children ______________ (7) (be) a bit older (up to ages 11 or 12) need from 9 to 13 hours per day. Teens have many adult characteristics, but their sleep habits are very different from adult sleep habits. Studies ______________ (8) (look) at teen sleep have shown that there is a physical reason for the extra sleep. The changes ______________ (9) (happen) in a teenager's body use up a lot of energy. Extra sleep helps renew energy.

2 Combine the two sentences about food and sleep. Make the second sentence a subject relative clause. Use *who* for people and *that/which* for things. Sometimes more than one answer is possible.

1. We eat certain kinds of food. These kinds of food affect our sleep.

   We eat certain kinds of food that/which affect our sleep.

2. There are some kinds of food. These kinds of food help people sleep.

   ____

3. Turkey is one example of a kind of food. This kind of food makes people sleepy.

   ____

4. Scientists say turkey contains tryptophan. The scientists study food.

   ____

5. Tryptophan is a chemical. This chemical leads to sleepiness.

   ____

6. Researchers say other kinds of food can keep you awake. The researchers study sleep problems.

   ____

7. Chocolate is one kind of food. This kind of food can make you stay awake.

   ____

More About Subject Relative Clauses

1 Complete the sentences with *that*, *who*, or *which* and the words in parentheses. Sometimes more than one answer is possible.

1. Tom is a sleepwalker. Sleepwalking is a disorder *that/which causes people to get up and walk* (cause / people / to get up and walk) during sleep.
2. For the last six months, he has been part of a group ______________________ (meet / weekly) to discuss their problems during sleep.
3. In the group, there are people ______________________ (walk / in their sleep) for years. They share stories and give advice.
4. There are people ______________________ (take / medication) every day to help them sleep better.
5. There are also people ______________________ (prefer / a more natural approach). They are doing relaxation exercises.
6. Walking outside while asleep is a problem ______________________ (concern / a lot of the group).
7. Tom also visits a website ______________________ (have / current information) and a discussion forum.

2 Complete the sentences with *whose* and the information in the chart. Use the words in parentheses to help you.

Sarah – friend	Ted – cousin	Pam – neighbor
parents / be sleep researchers	his uncle / sleep only five hours a night	her co-worker / study her dreams
her brother / talk in his sleep	his daughter / sometimes sleepwalks	her friends / like to stay up all night

1. Sarah's my friend *whose parents are sleep researchers* (sleep researchers).
2. Ted is my cousin ______________________________ (uncle).
3. Pam is my neighbor ______________________________ (co-worker).
4. Sarah's my friend ______________________________ (brother).
5. Ted is my cousin ______________________________ (daughter).
6. Pam is my neighbor ______________________________ (friends).

3 A Read the paragraph about people who sleep for long periods of time. Complete the sentences with the correct relative pronoun. Sometimes more than one answer is correct.

Rip Van Winkle

Louisa Ball

There is a classic American story about Rip Van Winkle. In the story, he is a man *who OR that* (1) sleeps for 20 years. Of course, Rip Van Winkle is not real. There is no real person __________ (2) has slept that long. However, there are many real people __________ (3) sleep times have amazed researchers. One is Louisa Ball. She's a young British woman __________ (4) has slept for as long as two weeks. She has a rare disease __________ (5) causes long periods of sleep. Another person with unusual sleep times is Randy Gardner. In 1964 he was a teenager __________ (6) went without sleep for 11 days. Having too little sleep is called *sleep deprivation*. Scientists __________ (7) have studied sleep deprivation know that it can affect a person's mind in strange ways. For example, sleep deprivation made Gardner think that he was a football player ________ (8) name was Paul Lowe. Gardner stayed awake by choice, as part of a science experiment. Other people have little control over their sleep times. They have diseases ________ (9) prevent sleep for weeks even though they want to sleep.

B Complete the sentences about the paragraph in A. Use the words in parentheses with *that, who,* and *whose.* Sometimes more than one answer is possible.

1. Rip Van Winkle is a character _that/who is in a story_ (a story / in / be).
2. Louisa Ball is a young woman ________________ (British / be).
3. Louisa has a disease ________________ (long / cause / sleep periods).
4. Randy Gardner was a young man ________________ (for 11 days / stay awake).
5. He was a teenager ________________ (sleep deprivation / be / part of a science project).
6. Sleep deprivation can cause problems ________________ (affect / your mind).
7. During his sleep deprivation, Randy thought he was someone ________________ (football / play).
8. Randy was unlike other people ________________ (come / from diseases / sleep deprivation).

Avoid Common Mistakes

1 Circle the mistakes.

1. Bob's the man **who** (a) slept during the meeting. Kathy is the person **which** (b) woke him up. Their boss is the person **that** (c) got angry.
2. Mice **who** (a) have a mutation need less sleep. Mice **that** (b) don't have the mutation sleep a normal amount. Humans might also have mutations **which** (c) affect sleep.
3. A team of researchers studied people **who are** (a) short sleepers. They have sleep patterns **that are** (b) unusual. They are sleepers **who they need** (c) only about six hours of sleep a night.
4. Doctors have some advice **that can help** (a) you sleep. Don't have any food or drinks **contain** (b) caffeine in the afternoon. Also, avoid activities **that take** (c) a lot of physical effort.

5. Children **who is** (a) 3 to 11 years old need at least 9 hours of sleep. Children **that are** (b) younger need even more sleep. Eighteen hours a day is normal for children **who are** (c) just babies.
6. This man is a scientist **whose research** (a) is about sleep. He has one assistant **whose college degree** (b) is in psychology. He has another assistant **who's field** (c) is medicine.
7. Dr. Shah runs a clinic **that** (a) treats sleep problems. He has an assistant **which** (b) has studied psychology. They help people **who** (c) have physical and psychological problems.
8. Researchers **who have studied** (a) sleep problems do hard work. The experiments **that they do** (b) require careful planning. The results **who come** (c) from these experiments are important.

2 Find and correct eight more mistakes in the article about driving while tired.

Tired Drivers in Danger

Josh Parker is a teacher ~~which~~ *who* often works late. He drives home on a dark road has no lights. A long workday, the late hour, and the dark road are a combination that it could be dangerous. Josh could fall asleep while driving and get into a bad accident. He admits that he is sometimes too tired to drive. "I am a guy who usually put safety first. I don't drink and drive, and I never drive at a speed is dangerous. Still, when I'm tired, I'm like a guy who's brain isn't working right." Josh has a problem who is very common. Like other people who is really tired, he sometimes makes bad decisions. When he feels tired, he should not drive by himself. He should drive with a friend who's role is to keep him awake.

Self-Assessment

Circle the word or phrase that correctly completes each sentence.

1. I have a friend _____ to stay awake for three days.

   a. tried b. who tried c. which tried

2. Researchers studied people. The people had sleep problems. Researchers studied people _____ sleep problems.

   a. whose studied b. who they had c. who had

3. People sometimes watch movies _____ too scary or exciting. Then they might have trouble sleeping.

   a. that   b. that are   c. that is

4. I know several people who _____ in a sleep study. They go to a sleep lab every day.

   a. are participating   b. is participating   c. participates

5. The police officer stopped a tired driver _____ almost went off the road.

   a. who's car   b. whose car   c. car that

6. A sleepwalker is someone _____ partly asleep and partly awake.

   a. who is brain   b. brain is   c. whose brain is

7. Some people have diseases _____ them awake for a long time.

   a. that keep   b. that   c. that they keep

8. My cousins _____ in New York sleep only about four hours a night.

   a. live   b. who lives   c. who live

9. Because Kate sleeps late, she is often late for her class _____ at 10:00 a.m.

   a. that starts   b. that start   c. that it starts

10. Don't try to wake up someone _____ sleepwalking.

    a. they are   b. who is   c. who are

11. A mouse _____ the hDEC2 gene needs less sleep than other mice.

    a. that has   b. that with   c. that it has

12. People _____ in their sleep have a very dangerous problem.

    a. which drive   b. who drives   c. that drive

13. There are road signs in Australia _____ drivers to take naps if they are tired.

    a. that   b. that tells   c. that tell

14. I'm a person _____ a favorite sleep position. I like sleeping on my back.

    a. who has   b. who have   c. who

15. Some sleepers _____ good dreams wake up happy and energetic.

    a. who's have   b. have   c. who have

UNIT 31

Object Relative Clauses (Adjective Clauses with Object Relative Pronouns)

Viruses

Object Relative Clauses

1 Complete the paragraph about viruses with *that*, *which*, or *who*. Sometimes more than one answer is possible.

For scientists, viruses are a puzzle _that OR which_ (1) they find difficult to solve. Is a virus a living thing or not? After more than a century of research, it is a question ________ (2) experts cannot answer. Most scientists used to think viruses were alive because they did things ________ (3) living things do. For example, one thing ________ (4) viruses and living things do is reproduce.[1] In the 1930s, however, the scientific view of viruses changed because of new discoveries ________ (5) scientists made. Pictures ________ (6) new microscopes[2] produced showed that viruses don't have many parts ________ (7) living cells need. Viruses are only pieces of DNA or RNA (chemicals for reproduction). Viruses can't produce the energy ________ (8) living things produce, so viruses have to stay inside living cells of people ________ (9) they've infected to survive. Some experts ________ (10) you can ask don't believe the theories ________ (11) these scientists have. They believe viruses are alive.

[1]**reproduce:** make new individuals with your genetic characteristics; humans reproduce by having children
[2]**microscope:** a piece of equipment that helps scientists look at very small things

2 Combine the sentences about colds and the flu with *that* or *which*.

1. The flu has some features. A cold does not have these features.

   The flu has some features _that/which a cold does not have_.

2. The two illnesses go through different cycles. Doctors have identified the different cycles.

   The two illnesses go through different cycles ________________________________.

3. The cycle for a cold is shorter than the cycle for the flu. Most people experience this cycle for a cold.

   The cycle for a cold ______________________ is shorter than the cycle for the flu.

4. With a cold, you might get a low fever. You will get over the fever in two or three days.

   With a cold, you might get a low fever ______________________.

5. With the flu, you may get a high fever. You may have this fever for seven to ten days.

   With the flu, you may get a high fever ______________________.

6. A cold might give you sore muscles. You can still use your muscles without a lot of pain.

   A cold might give you sore muscles ______________________.

7. The muscle soreness with the flu is more serious. You feel this soreness.

   The muscle soreness ______________________ with the flu is more serious.

8. There are other diseases, such as lung infections. The flu can lead to these diseases.

   There are other diseases, such as lung infections, ______________________.

More About Object Relative Clauses

1 Complete the article about how to prevent viruses. Use *that, which, who,* or Ø for no relative pronoun with the simple present, present perfect, or present perfect progressive form of the verbs in parentheses. Sometimes more than one answer is correct.

There is a lot of information about viruses *that* OR *which* OR *Ø* (1) scientists *have learned* (1) (learn) in the last few years. This is information ________ (2) we ________ (2) (use) every day to stay healthy and avoid disease. The most basic action ________ (3) we ________ (3) (do) every day to stay healthy is hand washing. Careful washing removes viruses before they can infect you. This is especially important when people ________ (4) you ________ (4) (interact) with a lot may have a virus.

Ads about hand washing ________ (5) health organizations ________ (5) (run) for many years have finally changed people's attitudes. If you cannot wash your hands when you leave your home, you can use a hand sterilizer ________ (6) stores and offices

now ________ (provide). This item is very important to have. Also, people
(6)

are now more aware of some advice ________ doctors ________ (give) for many years: If you're sick, stay home. Stay home for three days after getting a cold. You
(7) (7)

can infect people ________ you ________ (meet) during these three days.
(8) (8)

If you get a flu virus, you should stay away from your work for up to a week. Finally, most people know about vaccinations for the flu and other diseases ________ viruses ________ (cause).
(9) (9)

2 Combine the sentences with *that, whom,* or *whose.* Sometimes more than one answer is correct.

1. The Centers for Disease Control and Prevention (CDC) is a federal organization. The government created it to protect the health of people.

   The CDC is a federal organization that the government created to protect the health of people.

Great Grocery
Preferred Shopper Card

2. The CDC hires many people. The organization wants them to investigate health problems.

   ____

3. In the United States, 76 million people each year get sick from the food. They eat this food.

   ____

4. In 2010, hundreds of people became sick from a food. No one could identify the food.

   ____

5. Many of the sick people were from one state. Health officials investigated the sick people.

   ____

6. The health officials took the shopper cards. These people used these cards at grocery stores.

   ____

   ____

7. The shopper cards all had one food in common. Investigators identified this food as the source of the problem.

   ____

   ____

3 Complete the sentences with the words in parentheses.

1. Viruses lead to many diseases *whose causes scientists have wondered about* (causes / scientists / have / wondered about / whose).
2. Some of the illnesses ______ (cause / viruses / that) only last a short time.
3. People ______ (infect / who / most viruses) aren't sick for very long because their bodies quickly kill these viruses.
4. Long-term problems can come from illnesses ______ (cause / that / other viruses).
5. Illnesses ______ (serious / think / are / doctors / that) last a long time.
6. Dr. Harvey J. Alter is a doctor ______ (discovery in 1989 / of a virus / helped / whose) fight the chronic disease hepatitis C.
7. Until recently, hepatitis C was an illness ______ (could not cure / medicines / that).
8. However, a treatment ______ (doctors / have developed / recently / which) can cure some patients with hepatitis C.

Avoid Common Mistakes

1 Circle the mistakes.

1. Ms. Baker is the teacher **whom** (a) I like. Biology is the subject **who** (b) she teaches. Viruses are the topic **that** (c) we're studying.
2. A young boy was the person **who** (a) a dog bit. Pasteur was the doctor **who** (b) treated him. The boy was someone **who** (c) health Pasteur's vaccine helped.
3. Dr. Carter is someone **whom** (a) I don't like. Brian is my friend **whom** (b) sees Dr. Carter. Brian is someone **whom** (c) I worry about.
4. This is the medicine **that I take it** (a) when I have a cold. I keep it in a place **that I can easily reach** (b). However, it is also a place **that children can't reach** (c).
5. This is a vaccine **which** (a) the nurse sprays into my nose. It is a vaccine **which** (b) my doctor recommends. She is the doctor **which** (c) my whole family sees.

6. Dr. Rao is a famous doctor **who** (a) is on TV. He is also a writer **who** (b) books a lot of people read. He's the doctor **who's** (c) speaking at the college tonight.
7. Louis Pasteur was a researcher **whom** (a) most modern doctors admire. He was the one **whom** (b) developed a vaccine for rabies. Today is his birthday, December 27. He is the one **whom** (c) we remember today.
8. Many places **that people often touch** (a) can be full of viruses. Doorknobs and light switches are some objects **that viruses might be on** (b). One magazine article **that I read it** (c) emphasizes washing your hands after you touch these.

2 Find and correct eight more mistakes in the website for a college's health center.

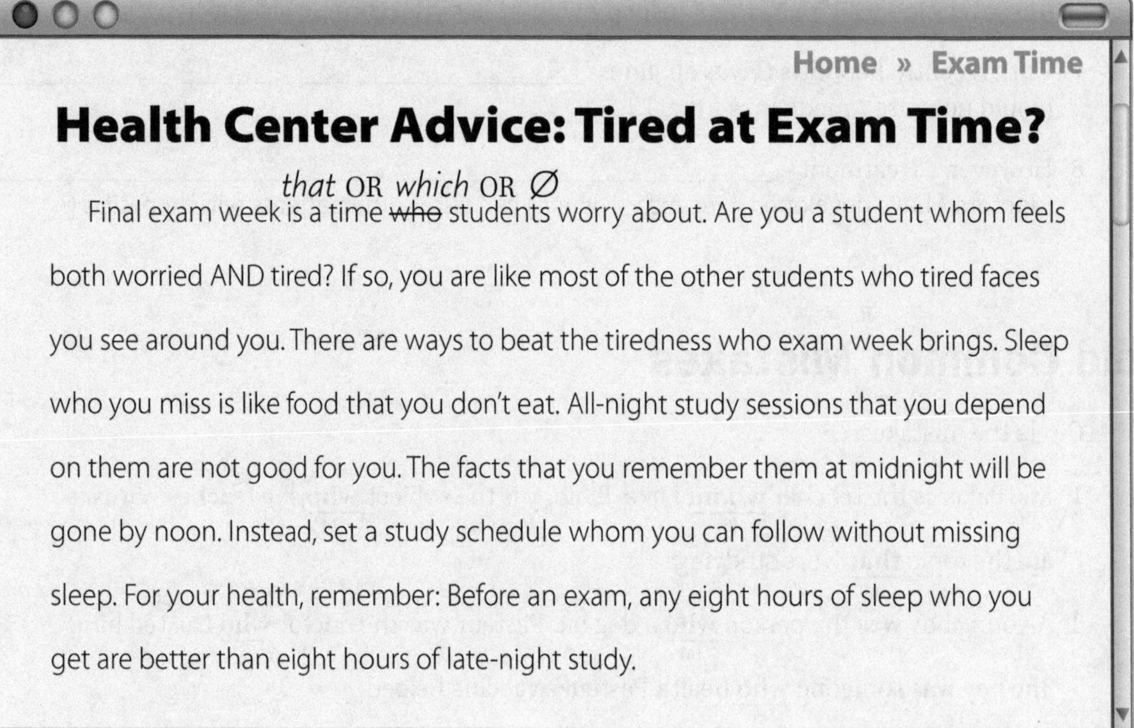

Home » Exam Time

Health Center Advice: Tired at Exam Time?

Final exam week is a time ~~who~~ *that* OR *which* OR ∅ students worry about. Are you a student whom feels both worried AND tired? If so, you are like most of the other students who tired faces you see around you. There are ways to beat the tiredness who exam week brings. Sleep who you miss is like food that you don't eat. All-night study sessions that you depend on them are not good for you. The facts that you remember them at midnight will be gone by noon. Instead, set a study schedule whom you can follow without missing sleep. For your health, remember: Before an exam, any eight hours of sleep who you get are better than eight hours of late-night study.

Self-Assessment

Circle the word or phrase that correctly completes each sentence.

1. There are many ways _____ to infect people.

   a. that travel viruses   b. that viruses travel   c. viruses travel that

2. If you have a cold, you could pass viruses to anything _____ .

   a. touch   b. that you touch it   c. that you touch

3. That is the illness. I caught the illness. That is the _____.

   a. illness I caught   b. illness who I caught   c. illness that caught

4. In 1918, the area _____ was the whole world.

   a. that   b. that affected the flu   c. that the flu affected

5. The doctor _____ knows a lot about the flu.

   a. who office I visited   b. whose office I visited   c. I visited her office

6. If someone _____ has a cold, don't shake hands with him or her.

   a. you know who   b. who   c. you know

7. The "Spanish flu" was a disease _____ more than 500 million people _____.

   a. that . . . caught   b. caught . . . that   c. that . . . who

8. There was a boy. A dog bit him. Pasteur treated his dog bite. There was a boy _____ Pasteur treated.

   a. who dog bite   b. whose dog bite   c. whom dog bite

9. Scientists have developed a vaccine _____ to avoid the flu.

   a. who people can get   b. whose people can get   c. that people can get

10. There are thousands of diseases _____.

    a. that viruses cause   b. who viruses cause   c. whom viruses cause

11. To avoid colds, Heather washes her hands often with a special soap _____ from her doctor.

    a. that she got   b. that got   c. that her got

12. The man _____ for SARS had just come back from a business trip.

    a. that treated   b. whose treatment   c. whom doctors treated

13. Children often come home with viruses _____.

    a. who other children got   b. that they from other children   c. that they got from other children

14. Anna has the flu. We need to wash all the surfaces _____.

    a. she touched   b. whom she touched   c. whose she touched

15. The advice _____ all my employees was, "If you're sick, don't come to work."

    a. that gave   b. that I gave   c. gave

UNIT 32

Conjunctions and Adverb Clauses

Special Days

Conjunctions

1 Complete the paragraph about holidays. Circle the correct conjunctions.

Do you celebrate National Grammar Day (March 4), Talk Like Shakespeare Day (April 23), **or / yet** (1) National Nothing Day (January 16)? A large percentage of people do not. They are actual holidays, **or / but** (2) very few people have heard of them. How do holidays like these start? In some cases, businesses want to sell more products, **or / so** (3) they invent a holiday for their products. For example, people in the food industry met **but / and** (4) created National Cranberry Day, National Carrot Day, and other days for fruits **so / and** (5) vegetables. Many of these invented holidays are not well known, **but / or** (6) some have become quite successful. For instance, Marian McQuade, a grandmother, invented National Grandparents Day (in early September), **and / or** (7) U.S. President Jimmy Carter made it a national holiday in 1978. National Talk Like a Pirate Day (September 19) is a very strange holiday, **yet / or** (8) many people celebrate it just for fun. Two friends, John Bauer **or / and** (9) Mark Summers, invented the holiday in 1995 as a joke. They sent a letter about it to a popular comedian, **and / but** (10) he promoted the holiday in his newspaper columns **and / yet** (11) on television. It became very popular. To celebrate it, people talk like the pirates in movies **so / and** (12) wear pirate clothes and pirate items like eye patches.

2 A Complete the article about the holiday Mardi Gras with *and, so,* or *but.* Add commas when necessary.

The holiday Mardi Gras has a French name <u>, but</u> (1) many Americans celebrate it. The name means "Fat Tuesday" in English. The holiday occurs on different dates every year ________ (2) it cannot be on just any date. The date is always somewhere between early February ________ (3) early March.

Mardi Gras is a very popular holiday. Many people like to attend celebrations ________ (4) many cities have celebrations. At these celebrations, people eat a lot of food, listen to music ________ (5) dance. Many cities celebrate Mardi Gras ________ (6) the city with the largest celebration is New Orleans, Louisiana. As many as half a million tourists come to New Orleans each year.

B Complete the end of the article with *or, so,* or *yet.* Add commas when necessary.

During Mardi Gras, people dress in costumes and wear masks. Often these costumes have a lot of feathers <u>or</u> (1) glitter. There are also large parades. These parades are now on the Internet ________ (2) people do not have to go to New Orleans to enjoy Mardi Gras. Many people watch the parades on the Internet ________ (3) the parades still have very large crowds. People watch the parades for the floats. Floats are vehicles that people decorate with flowers ________ (4) other plants. People ride the floats and throw things like toys, beads ________ (5) stuffed animals to people who are watching.

In August 2005, Hurricane Katrina destroyed much of New Orleans ________ (6) six months later, the city celebrated Mardi Gras. The celebration raised a lot of money for rebuilding the city ________ (7) it was important for helping the economy recover.

C Combine the sentences about Mardi Gras. Use *and, or, but, so,* and *yet.* Sometimes more than one answer is correct.

1. Some people call the holiday *Mardi Gras.* Other people call it *Fat Tuesday.*

   People call the holiday Mardi Gras or Fat Tuesday.

2. Mardi Gras is in February. Mardi Gras is in March. It is in one of these months each year.

   Mardi Gras is ________________________________ each year.

3. Many cities celebrate Mardi Gras. The best and largest celebration is in New Orleans.

   Many cities celebrate ________________________________

   ________________________________.

4. The people on the floats wear costumes. The people on the floats wear masks.

   The people on the floats ________________________________.

5. You can see the parades in New Orleans. You can see them on the Internet.

   You can see ________________________________.

6. As many as half a million people go to New Orleans each year for Mardi Gras. It is very crowded.

   As many as half a million people go ________________________________

   ________________________________.

7. Hurricane Katrina struck New Orleans in 2005. The city still celebrated Mardi Gras in 2006.

   Hurricane Katrina ________________________________

   ________________________________ in 2006.

Adverb Clauses

1 A Complete the paragraph about fall and winter holidays with *because* and *although.*

When we moved to the United States, we thought Halloween was a very strange holiday. I have learned to like it because (1) my children enjoy it very much. ____________ (2) I don't understand the reason for the holiday, the activities during this holiday are fun. My children teach me silly songs and poems about ghosts and witches. We make jack-o'-lanterns out of pumpkins. My children are very excited __________ (3) they can't wait to wear their costumes to school. Our town has a Halloween parade. I always participate __________ (4) I meet other parents. I like walking and talking to people __________ (5) I don't like all the candy that my children get from trick-or-treating.

B Complete the paragraph about winter holidays with *since* and *even though.*

I grew up in Michigan. Since (1) it is a northern state, the winters there are very cold and snowy. __________ (2) I grew up in a cold area of the country and I'm used to the cold, I have never liked the cold. I have also always hated wearing heavy clothes. During the holidays in the winter, I always preferred to stay inside __________ (3) I hated getting cold. My brothers and sisters couldn't wait for the first big snowfall, but I felt very differently. __________ (4) I found a good job after I graduated, I quit it and moved to Florida. My family was surprised. Now during the winter, I cheerfully sing holiday music and buy gifts, and I am much happier __________ (5) I can wear light clothes and have fun outside. Last year, my family visited me over the holidays. __________ (6) they missed the snow, they said that they loved the warm, sunny days.

2 Complete the sentences about summer holidays. Unscramble the adverb clauses. Use the correct form of the verbs.

1. begin / even though / summer / in June

   Even though summer begins in June, May 30, Memorial Day, is the official start of summer.

2. a three-day weekend / be / it / because / for many people

   Memorial Day is a favorite holiday ____________________.

3. people / barbecues / enjoy / all summer / although

   ____________________, July 4 is probably the most popular day to have them.

4. a patriotic holiday / be / since / July 4

   ______________________________________, people wave flags at parades.

5. because / come / in September / it

   People often feel that Labor Day is the end of summer ______________________________

   ____.

3 Answer the questions about holidays. Write sentences that are true for you.

1. Think of your favorite holiday. Why do you like it?

   I like *Thanksgiving* because *I get to eat a lot of good food* ____________.

2. What is something that you do during a holiday even though you don't like to do it?

   I ____________________ during ____________________ even though

   ____.

3. Think of an important holiday in your home country. Why do people celebrate it?

   People celebrate ______________ since ____________________________.

Avoid Common Mistakes

1 Circle the mistakes.

1. **Although the holidays make me feel stressed,** (a) I like them.
   Althought I always try hard, (b) I sometimes spend too much money.
   Although I like buying gifts, (c) I don't like spending too much money.

2. The Fourth of July is fun **even though the weather is sometimes very hot.** (a) I don't like Halloween **although it is fun it can be scary** (b). **Although the weather is cold,** (c) Christmas can be fun.

3. **Since Mark is Canadian** (a) he celebrates Canada Day.
   Although it is similar to the Fourth of July, (b) Canada Day is not about independence.
   Even though Canada is an independent country, (c) it still honors the Queen or King of Great Britain.

4. **Although the United States has 11 official holidays,** it celebrates many others. Mother's
(a)
Day is popular **even though it is not an official holiday most people celebrate it**.
(b)
Although the Friday before Easter is not an official holiday, some people do not have
(c)
to work that day.

5. **Even though Mother's Day is not an official holiday,** people celebrate it.
(a)
Even though they are far from home, young people call their mothers that day.
(b)
Because the holiday comes in May mothers often get flowers as gifts.
(c)

6. Card companies may make greeting cards for a holiday **althought it is not official**.
(a)
Although no parties are held on Grandparents Day, there are cards for it. There are
(b)
cards for Boss's Day **even though it's not an official holiday**.
(c)

7. Even though election days are not official holidays in the United States,
some people have the day off they go to vote.
(a)
Even though it is an important day, most Americans have to work.
(b)
Even though election day is not an official holiday in the United States, other
(c)
countries call it a holiday.

8. **Since people shop for gifts,** store owners like holidays.
(a)
Because people shop for a lot of gifts in December merchants like the winter
(b)
holidays the best. **Although Halloween is not as profitable as other holidays,** it is
(c)
still very good for businesses.

2 Find and correct eight more mistakes in the article about national holidays.

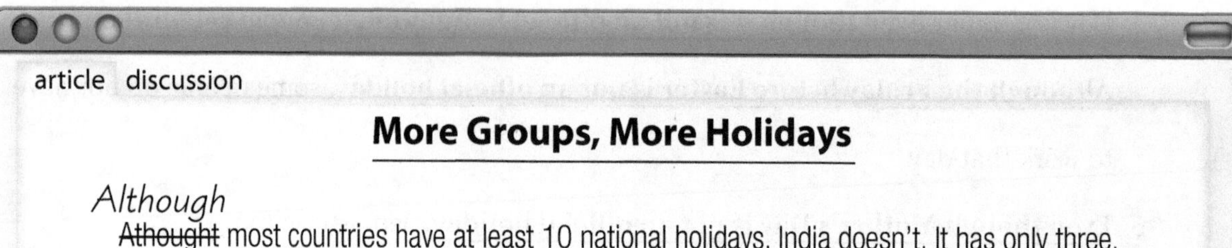

article discussion

More Groups, More Holidays

Although
~~Athought~~ most countries have at least 10 national holidays, India doesn't. It has only three. Because India has such a huge population you might be surprised. Since it has so many different ethnic and religious groups shouldn't it have more holidays? The answer is that it does although they are not national holidays they are celebrated in large areas of the country. Many countries have similar systems. Althought there are few national holidays, there are many important ones that are not official for the whole country. For example, because some U.S. states want to honor Abraham Lincoln they celebrate his birthday (February 12). Only four states have that holiday. State workers in Connecticut, Illinois, Missouri, and New York get the day off even though there is no national holiday no other states close government offices for that holiday. A small part of a state may celebrate a holiday althought the whole state doesn't celebrate it. Even though most cities in the state of Montana do not celebrate Chinese New Year, the city of Butte, Montana, has parades that day the city is home to many Chinese Americans.

Self-Assessment

Circle the word or phrase that correctly completes each sentence.

1. Both the United States _____ Canada celebrate a holiday called Thanksgiving.

   a. or b. and c. but

2. The holiday is in November in the United States _____ not in Canada.

   a. or b. so c. but

3. The weather is often bad in December, _____ many people still travel by car during the holidays.

   a. yet b. so c. or

4. You are welcome to visit us on Thanksgiving, Memorial Day, _____ any other holiday.

   a. so b. but c. or

5. Many people like to eat a lot on holidays, _____ I don't.

   a. and   b. or   c. but

6. On Halloween, many children dress up as _____ they go from house to house to get candy.

   a. monsters and   b. monsters, and   c. monsters but

7. The mall is enjoyable _____ exciting on Black Friday.

   a. and   b. but   c. and not

8. There is terrible traffic at the mall on holidays, _____ a lot of people want to go there.

   a. so   b. or   c. yet

9. Christmas holiday stories mention _____ it is a winter holiday.

   a. snow, because   b. snow because   c. snow,

10. Canada Day is Canada's national _____ is not about independence.

    a. day, although it   b. day. Although it   c. day, although

11. Since I live _____ can't visit my mother on Mother's Day.

    a. far away I   b. far away, I   c. far away,

12. Many stores are open on holidays _____ their workers would like to have the day off.

    a. so   b. even though   c. since

13. I bought a big _____ I have enough for our Thanksgiving dinner.

    a. turkey so   b. so turkey   c. turkey. So

14. _____ many people like to eat hot dogs on the Fourth of July, my family doesn't.

    a. Since   b. Althought   c. Although

15. My parents went to the mall at 8:00 a.m. _____ they were the first shoppers on Black Friday.

    a. so   b. yet   c. or

Art Credits

Illustration

Edwin Fotheringham: 10, 95, 100, 164; **Andrew NG:** 43, 106, 138, 146, 169; **John Kurtz:** 52, 158, 204; **Foo Lim:** 78, 95, 101, 110

Photography

2 *(l)* ©Elwynn*, *(r)* ©iStockphoto.com/STEEX; 12 Bruce Laurance/Getty Images; 13 iStockphoto.com/kali9; 16 ©iStockphoto.com/philsajonesen; 23 Jupiterimages/Getty Images; 24 Bloomberg via Getty Images; 29 DEA Picture Library/Getty Images; 31 *(l)* © Paul Orr*, *(r)* ©Neelsky*; 34 *(l)* Chris McGrath/Getty Images, *(r)* Mandel Ngan/AFP/Getty Images; 35 2011 STAR TRIBUNE/Minneapolis-St. Paul; 36 ©Kevin Tavares*; 37 David Karp/Ap Images; 50 Digital Globe/ZUMA/Corbis; 57 Bill Haber/AP Images; 59 Barry Austin/Getty Images; 64 Courtesy of Jet Propulsion Laboratory; 65 National Geographic/Getty Images; 66 Imagebroker.net/Superstock; 70 ©Tomaz Kunst*; 71 Jim Reed/Getty Images; 74 ©Sari Oneal*; 78 Andrew Watson/Photolibrary; 80 ©iStockphoto.com/wekeli; 81 Keith Bedford/Corbis; 84 Moodboard/Corbis; 88 Michael Maslan/Corbis; 92 Bill Varie/Corbis; 98 ©Paula Cobleigh*; 110 Newspix/Getty Images; 112 Yellow Dog Productions/Getty Images; 115 ©iStockphoto.com/4774344sean; 118 ©Shpilko Dmitriy*; 120 ©Susan Schmitz*; 124 Handout/Getty Images; 127 Filmmagic/Getty Images; 134 *(l)* ©iStockphoto.com/ArtisticCaptures, *(c)* ©Monkey Business Images*, *(r)* ©Stocklite*; 160 Corbis Super RF/Alamy; 166 ©iStockphoto.com/opulent-images; 171 Christopher Bissell/Getty Images; 176 Masterfile Royalty Free; 179 *(l)* ©Warren Goldswain*, *(r)* ©iStockphoto.com/billnoll; 184 *(t)*Reuters/Corbis, *(b)* ©iStockphoto.com/NetaDegany; 185 Comstock/Getty Images; 190 ©Korionov*; 193 Jose Luis Pelaez/Corbis; 197 Steve Hix/Getty Images; 198 *(t)* ©iStockphoto.com/tuncaycetin, *(b)* H. Armstrong Roberts/The Image Works; 204 Barcroft/Fame Pictures; 208 ©Sebastian Kaulitzki*; 209 ©topseller*; 214 Courtesy of The Pirate Guys LLC; 215 ©iStockphoto.com/dlewis33; 216 ©iStockphoto.com/wwing; 217 Floyd Dean/Getty Images.

*2011 Used under license from Shutterstock.com